PRAISE FOR *THE SOLOMON SEDUCTION*

The college and professional sports culture is very seductive on many levels. Mark offers a lot of practical, no-nonsense advice that will be a big help to athletes, but also anyone else trying to live a godly life. If you choose to dig into this book, make sure you have your highlighter ready!

DON DAVIS
TWO-TIME SUPER BOWL CHAMPION
DIRECTOR OF NFL PROGRAMS FOR PRO ATHLETES OUTREACH

The words explode off every page of Mark Atteberry's latest book, *The Solomon Seduction*. Get ready for a life-changing reading experience if your eyes are open, your mind is free and your heart is ready. This book is that impactful.

PAT WILLIAMS
ORLANDO MAGIC C-FOUNDER AND SENIOR VICE PRESIDENT
AUTHOR OF *COACH WOODEN'S GREATEST SECRET*

Mark has written another fantastic book. Ideal for sports teams, church men's groups, family men, or single guys, *The Solomon Seduction* speaks in a powerful way to the dangers we all face and the subtle, but deadly, power of seduction. I highly recommend it!

DOUG GOTCHER
FORMER NATIONAL CAMPUS DIRECTOR OF ATHLETES IN ACTION
CEO/PRESIDENT OF LEGACEE SYSTEMS

A must-read for all men in business and leadership positions.

PATRICK BET-DAVID
FOUNDER AND CEO, PEOPLE HELPING PEOPLE

Our ministry works with hundreds of church leaders and we've seen far too many "wise fools" fall. I cannot wait to give this book to Christian leaders around the country to help them recognize and address the seductions employed against them.

DARREN KEY

CEO, CHRISTIAN FINANCIAL RESOURCES

Mark's in depth character study of the life and many missteps of King Solomon is a powerful and much needed wake–up call for men. Through this book I have been reminded that the same old tricks the enemy used to trip up even the wisest of men in history are the ones he will use to make us fall today. These pages provide the practical steps we men can take to guard ourselves and keep our lives on the path to true wisdom.

MATTHEW WEST

CHRISTIAN RECORDING ARTIST

THE
SOLOMON
SEDUCTION

OTHER BOOKS BY MARK ATTEBERRY

The Samson Syndrome
The Climb of Your Life
The Caleb Quest
Walking with God on the Road You Never Wanted to Travel
The 10 Dumbest Things Christians Do
Free Refill
So Much More than Sexy
Let It Go
Dream (fiction)

THE
SOLOMON
SEDUCTION

WHAT YOU CAN LEARN FROM THE
WISEST FOOL IN THE BIBLE

MARK ATTEBERRY

W Publishing Group

An Imprint of Thomas Nelson

Published in Nashville, Tennessee, by W Publishing, an imprint of Thomas Nelson.

Author is represented by the literary agency of Alive Communications, Inc., 7680 Goddard Street, Suite 200, Colorado Springs, CO 80920, www.alivecommunications.com.

Thomas Nelson titles may be purchased in bulk for educational, business, fund-raising, or sales promotional use. For information, please e-mail SpecialMarkets@ThomasNelson.com.

Unless otherwise noted, Scripture quotations are taken from the *Holy Bible*, New Living Translation. © 1996, 2004, 2007 by Tyndale House Foundation. Used by permission of Tyndale House Publishers, Inc., Carol Stream, Illinois 60188. All rights reserved.

Scripture quotations marked NIV are from the Holy Bible, New International Version®, NIV®. Copyright © 1973, 1978, 1984 by Biblica, Inc.™ Used by permission of Zondervan. All rights reserved worldwide. www.zondervan.com.

Library of Congress Control Number: 2013922617

ISBN: 9780849964909

Printed in the United States of America
14 15 16 17 18 19 RRD 6 5 4 3 2 1

For Lee Hough

CONTENTS

Introduction xi

Historical Perspective xv

Author's Note xix

WAKE-UP CALL #1
  . . . Sin Seems Like a Good Idea   1

WAKE-UP CALL #2
  . . . God's Commands Seem Out of Touch   17

WAKE-UP CALL #3
  . . . Your Glory Is More Important to You than
  God's Glory   35

WAKE-UP CALL #4
  . . . You're More Influenced by Enticements
  than Warnings   51

TABLE OF CONTENTS

WAKE-UP CALL #5
... Sin Management Seems Like a Better Choice
than Repentance   69

WAKE-UP CALL #6
... Your Faithful Friends Are Troubled by
Your Behavior   87

WAKE-UP CALL #7
... Your Drinking Glasses Cost More than Some
People's Houses   105

WAKE-UP CALL #8
... There Are a Thousand Women Lined Up Outside
Your Bathroom   127

WAKE-UP CALL #9
... The Throne of Your Heart Goes from Being a
Chair to a Sofa to a Sectional   145

WAKE-UP CALL #10
... God Draws a Bull's-Eye on Your Chest   163

Afterword 179

A Message from Mark. 183

Study Guide 185

Acknowledgments 197

About the Author 199

Notes. 201

INTRODUCTION

IN 2003, I WROTE A BOOK CALLED *THE SAMSON SYNDROME*. IT WAS based on the life of a guy who might well be wearing a pair of blue tights and a red cape if he were alive today. Samson was the closest thing to a real-life Superman the world has ever seen. And he, too, had his Kryptonite: the curve of a woman's breast. It's what kept him in almost constant trouble, prevented him from fully accomplishing his God-given mission, and caused him to be humiliated at the end of his life.

In this book, I'm swinging the spotlight around and shining it on Solomon, probably the only guy in the Bible who could give Samson a run for his money when it comes to embarrassing moments. But don't get the idea that they were peas in a pod. Unlike Samson, Solomon didn't bench-press camels to impress the ladies. Instead, his most distinguishing muscle was between his ears. He was so wise that people came from all over the world to pick his brain. If he were alive today, he'd be writing self-help best sellers, taking questions from the audience on his own talk show, and giving motivational speeches to corporate conventions.

It seems impossible that the valedictorian of the entire human race would ruin his life by making dumb choices, but he did. In fact, I believe Solomon's demise was even more tragic than Samson's because his gift of wisdom was far more advantageous to spirituality than Samson's gift of physical strength. Solomon himself affirmed this in Proverbs 24:5 when he wrote, "The wise are mightier than the strong." Simply put, Solomon was better equipped to see through Satan's deceptions than any man who has ever lived, other than Jesus. But in the end, he became just as blind to them as everyone else.

This, of course, is quite a tribute to Satan's cleverness. If he were an author, his blockbuster best seller would be *How I Made a Fool Out of the Wisest Man Who Ever Lived (And Why the Program Still Works)*.

And it does still work. Pay attention to the news and you'll see that it's not just the numbskulls who fall into Satan's traps. It's also the best and brightest of America's fathers, husbands, and sons. I never cease to be amazed at how many smart guys who love God end up being shamed and humiliated by Satan's seductions. I bet you, too, could probably name four or five examples right off the top of your head.

That's why I wrote this book.

If you're a smart guy, an accomplished guy, a guy to whom people look for inspiration, leadership, and advice, I want to show you how Satan was able to seduce someone even sharper than you and offer some practical suggestions for how you can avoid a similar fate.

As usual, I intend to do all of this with humor and grace, because I despise all things heavy-handed and judgmental. I hate to be browbeaten, and I refuse to do so to others. That said, don't think for a moment that I'm going to play patty-cake with you. If you've read my other work, you know that's never the plan. This is far too serious a subject to take lightly. Every day, good men are waking up to the reality of life gone horribly wrong. They're finding themselves in circumstances they never envisioned, tangled up with people they never approved of, doing things they never imagined. They're seeing their reputations ruined, their loved ones devastated, their careers derailed, their futures clouded. And always, in the aftermath, with smoke rising from the rubble of their collapsed lives, they're asking, *What happened? How did I get here?* My goal is to help keep you (and me) from ever coming to that awful moment of devastated bewilderment. The only way to do that is to be frank and honest.

So buckle up and hold on tight. I'll be surprised if at least some of the chapters ahead don't give you a pretty good jolt. They sure did me when I was writing them.

HISTORICAL PERSPECTIVE

WHEN DAVID AND BATHSHEBA CAME TOGETHER FOR THEIR FIRST night of illicit sex, they conceived a son who died in infancy. Their second son lived. They named him Solomon, which means "peaceful," perhaps because, after all the dirty dealing that facilitated their coming together, their lives had finally settled down and become just that. But God chose a nobler name for the child: Jedidiah, which means "loved by the Lord" (2 Sam. 12:25).

Little is known about Solomon's childhood. We do know that he assumed his father's throne when he was about twenty and that one of his first official acts was to execute some of his father's old enemies who were lurking in the shadows, just waiting to cause trouble. It was a gutsy move, carried out on the advice of his dying father, and it proved to be a wise one. Solomon would have found it impossible to establish himself as king and earn the respect of the people with so many troublemakers actively plotting his demise.

As a young king, Solomon loved the Lord (1 Kings 3:3). On

one occasion, he went to Gibeon and offered a thousand sacrifices. That night, the Lord appeared to him in a dream and invited him to ask for anything he wanted. Solomon asked for wisdom, and God, thoroughly pleased, gave him a heaping helping (1 Kings 3:10–12). From that point on, Solomon was a fountain of brilliance. He wrote 3,000 proverbs, composed 1,005 songs, and spoke with encyclopedic authority on virtually every subject imaginable. He was so respected that kings from every nation sent their ambassadors to ask him questions (1 Kings 4:32–34).

Both Solomon and his father were prolific writers and wealthy kings, but don't get the idea that Solomon was a chip off the old block. David was primarily a warrior, while Solomon was primarily a politician. Even more significant is the fact that David, for all his imperfections, trusted God throughout his life, while Solomon trusted more in his ability to negotiate a good treaty.

And that's what got him into trouble.

Once he embraced negotiation and compromise as the main tenets of his foreign policy, things went downhill in a hurry. Instead of trusting the God who had promised to protect and defend Israel from all her enemies (Deut. 33:29), Solomon started negotiating treaties and business deals with surrounding nations. This led to some overcrowding in the royal bedroom as Solomon's wheeling and dealing netted him a mindboggling seven hundred wives and three hundred concubines. But the real trouble started when those ladies showed up on the palace steps lugging not only their suitcases but their gods. Suddenly, the palace was filled with idols, and it was only a matter of time before Solomon's heart was turned away from the God of his youth (1 Kings 11:4).

Solomon's reign lasted forty years, from 970 until about 931 BC. During that time, he expanded Israel's borders and enlarged the government. He also accumulated unimaginable wealth and experienced every pleasure that held even the slightest interest

(Eccl. 2:8). His crowning achievement was the building of a magnificent temple in Jerusalem, which was Israel's first permanent house of worship. But none of this led to happiness and fulfillment. The book of Ecclesiastes, which most scholars believe he wrote near the end of his life, reeks of sadness and regret. In addition, he left his people overtaxed, overworked, unhappy, and in spiritual decline.

I often wonder if Satan considers Solomon's sad demise to be his *Mona Lisa*. I wouldn't blame him if he did. Never has a man with the potential to soar so high sunk so low. In the end, it happened because Solomon didn't take his own advice: "Guard your heart above all else, for it determines the course of your life" (Prov. 4:23).

AUTHOR'S NOTE

SEDUCTION IS THE ART OF ENTICING A PERSON TO MAKE NEGATIVE behavioral choices he or she would otherwise avoid. The first seduction happened in the garden of Eden when Satan enticed Eve to eat the forbidden fruit. The second happened a few minutes later when Eve held the fruit up to Adam, smacked her lips, moaned, and said, "Man, this is good! Here, try some!" (Gen. 3:1–6).

A few of the more famous seducers in the Bible would include Jacob (Gen. 25:27–34), Potiphar's wife (Gen. 39:6–12), Delilah (Judg. 16:4–20), and David (2 Sam. 11:2–5). Outside the Bible, people like Cleopatra, Casanova, Marilyn Monroe, and even a fictional character like James Bond both epitomize and glorify the art of seduction.

But other people aren't always the cause of one's seduction. For example, there's no single person you can point to as the agent of Solomon's demise. He was seduced by privilege, power, riches, and the accolades of others. That's probably why he didn't realize what was happening. If it had been a matter of a beautiful woman disrobing in front of him, I feel confident he would have put two and two together. But because there was no seductress, and because it was a gradual process that unfolded over the length of his forty-year reign, it was easy for him just to lie back and let the current carry him along.

If you are being seduced, the thing you need more than anything else is what Solomon apparently never got: a wake-up call. I intend for each of the following chapters to ring loud and clear, to shake you, wake you, and make you see the reality of your situation.

WAKE-UP CALL №1

YOU KNOW YOU'RE BEING SEDUCED
WHEN SIN SEEMS LIKE A GOOD IDEA

I HATE SNAKES, PROBABLY MORE THAN ANYBODY YOU'VE EVER MET.
I know I should value their contribution to the ecosystem. I'm
well aware that their venom is used to advance medical research.
And I admit it would be nice to have a pet that doesn't bark or
require me to follow along behind it with a pooper-scooper. Still,
I hate snakes. They flat out give me the creeps.

This being the case, you can imagine how squeamish I got
when I saw *Raiders of the Lost Ark*. Remember when Indy and
Marion are in the Well of Souls and are surrounded by what looks
like hundreds, if not thousands, of snakes? Indy falls down, only
to look up and find himself staring into the beady eyes of a giant
cobra. At that moment, even as I sat there in the theater, Harrison
Ford was inducted into my own personal hall of fame. I thought,
*Dude, you have to be the bravest man on the planet. Are they really
paying you enough to film this scene?*

But wait!

What was that I saw?

If you watch closely, you'll see a quick reflection as Indy waves a torch at the snake. It turns out that he was never in any danger because they filmed the scene with a large pane of glass separating him from the cobra.[1]

This is yet another example of how deceiving appearances can be. Or, to be blunt, how easy we are to fool, even though the machinery that sits inside our skulls is amazing. Did you know that your brain contains a network of about 100,000 miles of blood vessels and 100,000,000,000 (one hundred billion) neurons with the ability to perform ten quadrillion operations per second? Or, to put it another way, imagine the scope and complexity of every telephone system in the world combined. Each individual brain cell you possess embodies that kind of functioning capacity.[2]

Yet, even with all that muscle between our ears, we are easily duped. All Steven Spielberg had to do was have the stagehands carry in a large pane of glass, and millions of people walked out of the theater, shaking their heads in wonder and talking about how ol' Harrison Ford sure does have a lot of guts.

Obviously, Satan is delighted by our extreme dupability. It means that every man on earth—regardless of his intelligence— is ripe for seduction. A little trick here, a little sleight of hand there, and even the sharpest guys will believe a lie and go skipping merrily down the road to shame and humiliation.

It happened to Solomon shortly after he became king.

His first order of business was to eliminate some of his father's old enemies, a band of bitter, unscrupulous men who were itching to undermine his authority and steal the kingdom. Removing them was a smart move. With those shady characters out of the way, Solomon was able to settle in and relax. First Kings 2:46 says, "So the kingdom was now firmly in Solomon's grip."

A few verses later we're told that Solomon loved the Lord and followed all the instructions of his father, David. We're also told that he went to Gibeon (where the tabernacle was located) and offered a thousand sacrifices. Solomon's first days in office appear to have been a roaring success.

Except for one thing.

You might miss it if you're not paying close attention.

Right in the middle of all this glowing information about the young king, we find these words: "Solomon made an alliance with Pharaoh, the king of Egypt, and married one of his daughters" (1 Kings 3:1). Only sixteen words, but they speak volumes. They tell us that the seduction of Solomon is officially under way.

You see, God's law strictly forbade all Israelites, whether peasants or kings, from marrying foreign women. Deuteronomy 7:3–4 says, "You must not intermarry with them. Do not let your daughters and sons marry their sons and daughters, for they will lead your children away from me to worship other gods." Don't think for a second that Solomon didn't know this law. It would have been drilled into him since he was young. Yet somehow, taking a foreign wife still looked like a great idea.

Many scholars believe that Solomon did not propose or initiate this alliance with Egypt. They theorize that after he got rid of his political enemies and secured his grip on the kingdom, his stature increased on the world stage. Foreign leaders recognized that he was an up-and-coming force to be reckoned with and thought it would be wise to be his friend rather than his enemy. In all likelihood, Pharaoh proposed the alliance and offered his daughter's hand in marriage. Solomon was flattered by the offer and found it easy to rationalize his acceptance. He probably said, "This is a no-brainer. It'll help to ensure peace and security for years to come." He was even thoughtful enough to keep his new Egyptian wife away from the palace so her presence wouldn't taint the holiness of the place (2 Chron. 8:11). He seemed to have it all figured out. His advisers probably congratulated him on an excellent deal. (I can even imagine them elbowing him in the ribs and winking if the girl happened to be a knockout.)

But it was still a sin, and it was only the tip of the iceberg.

Years later, Solomon would have a thousand foreign women roaming the palace grounds. Even worse, he would be worshipping their gods. The very thing God had warned against would be reality.

SATAN'S BEST TRICK

Right here, at the beginning of Solomon's story, we get a crystal-clear picture of Satan's best trick. (Best, that is, from his perspective.) Of all the nasty little stunts he pulls, making sin look like a good idea is easily the most dastardly. You've heard the old saying about how putting lipstick on a pig doesn't change the fact that it's a pig and certainly doesn't fool anybody. Well, Satan would beg to differ. He's found that by putting a little lipstick on certain sins, he can totally bamboozle a lot of perfectly intelligent guys.

Let me mention some of the "lipsticks" he uses . . . things that cause terrible sins to appear harmless or even attractive.

LIPSTICK #1: ALCOHOL

That great theologian Mickey Gilley had a hit song about how the girls in a bar all get prettier around closing time. According to the Mick, that old hag you wouldn't look at twice under normal circumstances suddenly starts looking like a Las Vegas showgirl when you get your belly full of booze.

He's right, of course. The world looks different when you're liquored up. Stupid things suddenly look smart. Like punching your wife, screaming profanity at your kids, driving thirty miles an hour above the speed limit, gambling away your paycheck, hiring a hooker, or flirting with your best friend's wife. You don't have to watch the evening news for five minutes before you'll see the mug shot of some droopy-eyed drunk who just ruined his life by doing something he never would have done if he'd been sober. No wonder Paul said, "Don't be drunk with wine, because that will ruin your life" (Eph. 5:18).

LIPSTICK #2: PRIVACY

Second only to alcohol in terms of its power to make the taboo tempting is privacy. When you think no one is looking—when you're pretty sure you can indulge and not get caught—the seductive power of any temptation ramps up significantly.

And sin brokers understand this. Why do you think most adult video stores and strip clubs have fenced-in parking lots located strategically behind the building? Why do you think companies that mail pornographic materials to your home do so in plain packaging? Why do you think software companies invest millions in creating programs that enable you to erase your online footprints? And why do you think hotels offer payment options that enable you to watch pornographic movies in your room without the charge showing up on your bill?

The world calls this sort of thing *discretion*.

Satan calls it *bait*.

He's trying to get you to "bite," and he knows that the promise of privacy will help allay your biggest fear: getting caught.

LIPSTICK #3: FINANCIAL BENEFIT

"But I need the money."

"The money's too good."

"Where else can I make this kind of money?"

These are just a few of the responses I've gotten from people

I've talked to who've been involved in questionable activities. One fellow was rationalizing the dishonest sales tactics he was required to use by his money-obsessed boss. A young woman was explaining why she allowed herself to be objectified as a Hooters girl. Another young man was working as a bartender even though he'd had a close friend who was killed by a drunk driver. They all had misgivings about what they were doing but felt that the financial benefit was just too significant to walk away from.

Paul said, "The love of money is at the root of all kinds of evil. And some people, craving money, have wandered from the true faith and pierced themselves with many sorrows" (1 Tim. 6:10).

LIPSTICK #4: POPULAR OPINION

This is likely where Solomon went wrong. It was common in those days for rulers to strike business deals and negotiate peace treaties that involved the swapping of daughters. What better way to ensure lasting peace between neighbors? So when Pharaoh came up with just such a proposal, Solomon's advisors probably fell all over themselves encouraging him to accept. They probably said, "This is great! It means he's taking you seriously as a world leader! You need to accept this deal and prove to him that you understand how the game is played!"

In our time, many sins have lost their stigma and become widely accepted because of changes in public opinion. Take cohabitation, for example. I can remember when it was considered scandalous for two people to live together outside of marriage. Now, it's not only accepted but thought by many (including a lot of Christians) to be a wise strategy for determining compatibility or saving money before the wedding. I've had young couples look at me as if I were from Mars because I dared to challenge their living arrangements. "But everybody does it" is a common refrain.

In addition to putting themselves at odds with God, these individuals fail to recognize the damage they're doing to the credibility of the body of Christ. Like Solomon of old, they miss the point that we have no meaningful witness if we're just like everybody else. That's why God said, "Come out from among unbelievers, and separate yourselves from them . . . Don't touch their filthy things" (2 Cor. 6:17).

LIPSTICK #5: MODERATION

This refers to the age-old notion that it's okay to drink as long as you don't get drunk. It's okay to gamble as long as you don't invest more than you can afford to lose. And of course, the biggie—the line that millions of teenage boys have tried on their girlfriends: "It's okay to fool around as long as we don't go all the way."

Don't misunderstand. Moderation can be a great thing. But the idea that anything is okay as long as it's done in moderation has given rise to some of the wackiest notions known to man. For example, you may have heard the term "technical virgin." It refers to someone who's done every sexual thing there is to do, except intercourse. (Remember, it was Bill Clinton who taught us that oral sex isn't really sex.) So when you ask this person if he or she is a virgin, the answer is, "I've never actually gone all the way, so, *technically*, yes."

One of the big problems with using moderation as a justification for whatever you want to do is that it's almost impossible to take just a bite when you're really hungry. Solomon, for example, was obviously hungry for power and influence on the world stage, so one treaty and one foreign wife were never going to be enough. One good bite (treaty) led to another and another and another until he ended up with a thousand foreign women in his harem.

LIPSTICK #6: PEER PARTICIPATION

You've heard of peer pressure. Peer participation is a little different. It's the pull you feel when you see one of your peers participating in a questionable activity, even though he or she may not be pressuring you to jump in. Just the fact that someone you know and respect is indulging legitimizes the activity and makes it easier for you to rationalize your own participation.

It also gives you a line of defense if you get caught. As long as you can point to some halfway respectable person who also does what you did, you will have at least one leg to stand on, feeble though it may be.

This is one of the main reasons why I don't drink alcohol. I'm well aware that the Bible doesn't condemn drinking, only drunkenness. Further, I recognize that every Christian has to wrestle with this issue and come to his own conclusion. Nevertheless, I believe that if I, as a pastor, were to be seen drinking alcohol, or even buying it at the supermarket, that could legitimize it in someone's mind—someone who might someday develop a drinking problem. In order to take that possibility off the table, I simply choose not to drink alcohol at all.

OUR BEST DEFENSE

The other day I signed on to my AOL account and saw a link urging me to check out some high-profile female celebrities without their makeup. With this chapter's lipstick motif swimming around in my head, I couldn't resist. I won't name names, but honestly, some of the pictures were truly frightening. I immediately stopped and offered a prayer of thanks for Revlon, COVERGIRL, and Estée Lauder.

But it got me thinking.

How different would this world be if we could see through all the makeup? Without the ability to hide their physical flaws, would certain female celebrities who are marginally talented (or not talented at all) have ever become famous? And what about sin? If we could see beyond the aforementioned lipsticks, would certain temptations suddenly be a lot easier to resist? I think they would, which is why I am a big believer in a little thing called *discernment*. It is our best defense against Satan's best trick.

Discernment is simply the ability to see beyond the lipstick. It's the ability to look at something—a person, a path, a proposition—and see it for what it really is, regardless of how much someone has tried to pretty it up. If you look up the word in your Bible's concordance, you'll find only a handful of references and maybe get the idea that God didn't say much about discernment. But if you understand that the words *wisdom, understanding,* and *good judgment* are interchangeable with *discernment,* you'll realize that the Bible is chock-full of insights and exhortations on this subject. The book of Proverbs, for example (much of which, ironically, was written by our boy Solomon), is about discernment from start to finish. In fact, the book opens with these words:

These are the proverbs of Solomon, David's son, king of Israel.

Their purpose is to teach people wisdom and discipline,
    to help them understand the insights of the wise.
Their purpose is to teach people to live disciplined and successful lives,
    to help them do what is right, just, and fair.
These proverbs will give insight to the simple,
    knowledge and discernment to the young. (Prov. 1:1–4)

I can't think of a better place to spend the remainder of this chapter than in the book of Proverbs. If we're serious about seeing "beyond the lipstick," we need to understand three essential truths about discernment.

ESSENTIAL TRUTH #1: DISCERNMENT MUST BE ACQUIRED

Review the opening passage of Proverbs quoted above and you'll see that the entire emphasis is on acquiring the discernment needed to live "disciplined and successful lives" and to "do what is right, just, and fair." There is an unspoken understanding that no one is born with discernment.

How else could we have developed such an elaborate Santa Claus myth? The very notion that a man with flying reindeer could deliver a toy to every good little boy and girl on earth in a single night is patently absurd. Yet little children continue to believe it with all their hearts, especially those whose parents encourage them to write letters to Santa and leave milk and cookies for him to snack on when he stops by. Small children fall for such an outlandish hoax because they are born with zero discernment.

Even older kids who have figured out that there is no Santa Claus can be tricked, like my childhood chum who was left standing in the middle of nowhere with a burlap bag, waiting for the older boys who left him there to chase a snipe in his direction. It took him awhile, but he finally figured out that he'd been duped, that there is no such thing as a snipe, and that said older boys were all back at the house laughing their mischievous heads off. Was he embarrassed? You bet. But he was also a little smarter for his trouble.

But figuring out that there's no such thing as a snipe or that Santa Claus is a myth is a far cry from developing the kind of discernment that will keep you from stumbling into one of Satan's traps. Getting to the place where you can see beyond Satan's lipsticks takes work. Solomon himself said, "Wisdom is always distant and difficult to find" (Eccl. 7:24). Only those who really apply themselves will acquire it.

ESSENTIAL TRUTH #2: DISCERNMENT IS ACQUIRED THROUGH THE STUDY OF GOD'S WORD

Granted, if you never picked up a Bible from the day you were born until the day you died, you'd still gain a certain amount of discernment. This fallen world will plant the toe of its boot squarely upon your hindquarters from time to time and you *will* learn valuable lessons. Thankfully, God offers us a less painful way to gain discernment. Proverbs 2:6 says, "The LORD grants wisdom! From his mouth come knowledge and understanding." If you get into the Word and soak up God's wisdom, you may still feel the impact of that pesky boot from time to time, but those occasions will most certainly be fewer in number and less painful. Proverbs 28:26 says, "Anyone who walks in wisdom is safe." Not pain free, but safe.

Tragically, very few men are deeply into the Word of God. I don't have a stat for you, but the "eyeball test" tells me it's true. I see how the women outnumber the men, not just in our church services Sunday after Sunday, but in the churches where I speak. I see how hard it is to get large numbers of men to show up for a prayer breakfast, a Bible study, or a small group. I see how the average Christian bookstore will devote only a couple of shelves to men's titles and ten times that many to women's titles. (Publishers and bookstore owners know better than anyone who is reading and who isn't!) And I see more and more churches limping along with shallow, marginally committed male leadership.

A few years ago, I spoke at a men's retreat where one of the organizers of the event picked me up at the airport. As we drove to the retreat center he bubbled over with enthusiasm about all the preparations that had been made. He said, "We've done everything we can think of to get the guys to come." And they had. They were offering a free rib-eye steak dinner, a live band, door prizes, a "goodie bag" full of free books and restaurant coupons, and a deeply discounted round of golf on a spectacular course. As we rode back to the airport the next evening, the same man lamented what he felt was a poor turnout. In an effort to lighten his mood, I jokingly suggested that maybe it was the speaker (me) that kept the guys away. As soon as the comment was out of my mouth, I regretted it as the thought struck me that maybe I *was* the reason for the poor attendance. He graciously assured me that was not the case and then added, "I don't know what it is with guys. It's just so hard to get them interested in the things of God."

What about you? Are you a guy who has to be bribed with a steak or a round of golf before you'll invest time and energy in spiritual growth? Are you a guy who is happy to flip burgers at the church picnic or help with repairs to the church roof but would never think of sitting down in a quiet place with a Bible and really checking out what God has to say? Bottom line: are you just a guy who goes to church, or are you serious about growing spiritually and acquiring discernment?

Satan's chances of seducing you will rise or fall on your answers to these questions.

ESSENTIAL TRUTH #3: DISCERNMENT DOESN'T WORK AUTOMATICALLY

Solomon is the perfect example of the fact that you can have your cranium crammed full of discernment and still end up embarrassing yourself. Keep in mind, he not only *knew* the book of Proverbs, he *wrote* the vast majority of it! And then ended up doing many of the very things he himself said were foolish!

Of course, Solomon is not alone in this regard. Every day seems to bring some new report about a perfectly intelligent man doing something he knows good and well is off-the-charts stupid, like Brett Favre sending sexually charged text messages to a woman who was not his wife. Or former US congressman Anthony Weiner posting vulgar pictures of himself on Twitter. The lesson here is that discernment doesn't work like central air-conditioning. You can't just set your wisdom thermostat at a certain level and then forget about it, trusting it to turn on and off as needed. Instead, wisdom works more like the blade on a riding mower.

Many years ago a teenage boy in our congregation volunteered to mow the church lawn. More accurately, he was in trouble at home, and mowing the church lawn was, in his opinion, the least traumatic of all the punishment options his dad allowed him to choose from. At any rate, I walked out of the church office to run an errand, and he happened to be cruising by. He slammed on the brake and motioned for me to come over. Above the roar of the engine he informed me that the mower blade really needed to be sharpened because it wasn't cutting well. I looked down and realized that he hadn't engaged the blade, which meant he'd been riding all over the property on what amounted to a sightseeing trip. You can imagine how embarrassed he was when I calmly reached down and pulled the lever that caused the blade to start spinning and grass to start flying.

Discernment, like a riding mower blade, can be razor sharp and well oiled, but the only way it's going to help you is if you engage it. That's why Solomon urged us to not forget wisdom (Prov. 3:1), turn our backs on wisdom (Prov. 4:6), let go of wisdom (Prov. 4:13), lose sight of wisdom (Prov. 4:21), or stray from wisdom (Prov. 5:7). These exhortations are clearly aimed at people who already have wisdom, indicating that having it and using it are two different things. Solomon would be the first to admit that, as the subtitle of this book suggests, it's possible to be a wise fool.

HOW DUPABLE ARE YOU?

Right now would be a good time for you to calculate your dupability quotient.

First, list the things you've done that would qualify as both unquestionably sinful and exceedingly dumb, even if you didn't get caught. (If this takes more than five minutes, you can skip the rest of the formula and simply pronounce yourself a fool.)

Second, answer this question: When enticed by sin, do you think first of Bible verses (0 points), people you know who've committed the sin in question without suffering terrible consequences (2 points), ways you just might be able to get away with it (3 points), or reasons why the rules are different for you (4 points)?

Third, give yourself one point for every time your dumb behavior has put you in a situation where you needed to apologize or make restitution.

Fourth, give yourself two points for every time your dumb behavior has gotten you injured, fired, suspended, expelled, sued, or served with divorce papers.

Finally, give yourself three points for every time you've been arrested.

Now add up your score.

Obviously, a perfect score would be zero. If you scored zero you're either Jesus Christ, dishonest, or in denial.

If you scored four or less, you're a tough nut for Satan to crack. Congratulations.

If you scored between four and eight, you need to step up your game before you seriously mess up your life.

If you scored higher than eight, you probably have both an attorney and a bail bondsman on speed dial.

You may scoff at an exercise like this, but you can be sure

Satan knows precisely how dupable you are. He may not calculate an actual number, but you can bet he has you labeled as someone who is worth spending time on or not. James said, "Resist the devil, and he will flee from you" (James 4:7). Does Satan flee from people because he is scared? No, he flees because he knows a waste of time when he sees one.

The word *discernment* doesn't appear in James 4:7. But make no mistake: it's there. All resistance to Satan begins with discernment. You may ultimately have other reasons for choosing not to give in to temptation (such as your love for God), but your initial hesitation is always going to be fueled by your suspicion that there's a pig behind all that lipstick.

So what is your dupability quotient?

Is it a number that sends Satan on his way or one that causes him to lick his chops?

Throughout my life I've heard people say, "Never say never!" And every time something truly unlikely happens, it seems like good advice. (Cubs fans, take heart!) But there is at least one sentence I can think of where the word *never* is absolutely the proper word to use: Sin is *never* a good idea. Even if you can envision how the greater good could be accomplished by just a tiny bending of God's rules, slam on the brakes and go no further. Remind yourself that Solomon's trouble started with a compromise that seemed to serve the greater good.

I can just imagine the celebration Solomon and his advisors had when the treaty with Egypt was signed. There must have been a lot of backslapping and chest thumping as they raised their glasses in a toast and congratulated themselves. And all the while Satan was smiling. He knew the playing field had just tilted in his favor. I can just imagine him turning to his executive assistant demon and saying, "Game on!"

I'll say it again.

Sin is never a good idea.

By acknowledging this truth and keeping it in the forefront of your mind, you will render Satan's lipsticks ineffective and make yourself very difficult to seduce.

WAKE-UP CALL №2

YOU KNOW YOU'RE BEING SEDUCED WHEN GOD'S COMMANDS SEEM OUT OF TOUCH

I HATE TO GIVE SATAN PROPS, BUT IT'S FOOLISH TO PRETEND HE isn't good at what he does. Take this seduction business, for example. Almost every man he sets his sights on has several good reasons to fight him tooth and nail. A husband, for example, need only look at the third finger of his left hand to be reminded of his marriage vows. He might also have children, a home, or a career he could lose if he did something foolish. And that's not to mention his upbringing, which often amounts to years and years of lectures, spankings, groundings, observations of other people's mistakes, and self-inflicted traumas, all of which point toward the wisdom of behaving oneself. Yet, day after day, Satan maneuvers over, under, and around these positive incentives and seduces more good men.

I've read books about Satan's strategies written by highfalutin scholars. I've heard sermons about Satan's strategies delivered by dynamic megachurch pastors. Sadly, I've then seen some of those same scholars and pastors turn right around and fall under the spell of the very enemy they sought to expose. My conclusion is that none of us have our enemy totally figured out. He's more adept than even the sharpest among us can fathom, which is why I think this book is so important. It's not about outsmarting Satan. It's about knowing what to look for.

If you think about it, knowing what to look for is the key to success in many areas of life.

For example, I can't read my wife's mind, but I've picked up on certain signals that tell me she's unhappy.

I am no financial expert, but I can look at the interest a bank offers and the fees they charge and figure out if they're offering me a good deal.

I've never studied oncology, but I know the seven symptoms cancer can produce.

Likewise, I don't know when or how Satan might try to seduce me, but I know to keep my eyes peeled for the classic warning signs that cropped up in Solomon's life. And one of those key warning signs is that Solomon began acting as though God's Word was out of touch with his real-world experience.

From the very beginning of our faith journey, our pastors, mentors, and Christian friends drill into us: Read your Bible. Study your Bible. Trust your Bible. Why? Because "all Scripture is God-breathed and is useful for teaching, rebuking, correcting and training in righteousness" (2 Tim. 3:16 NIV). We're talking Christianity 101 here. Nothing is more basic or more essential, and Satan knows it.

That's why all of Satan's various attempts at seducing believers must include an attempt to undermine Scripture. He might attack one man in the area of lust, another in the area of greed, and yet another in the area of ambition. Each attack will have its own unique features depending on the circumstances, personality, and maturity of the target, but every attack will have to reckon with the Word of God because Scripture is a Christian's first line of defense.

Think of a burglar. The whole key to his success is being able to get past the locks. There might be a dozen variables he will have to contend with from job to job, but he will always have to get past the locks.

Again, I have to grudgingly give Satan some credit. Like a skilled burglar, he understands that his best chance for success is to slip in and out unnoticed. Why blow a hole in the door if you can pick the lock? Why waste your time trying to discredit the whole Bible when all you need is for your target to relax his attitude toward one little command?

In recent years atheists have put on their game faces and become very aggressive. Men like Christopher Hitchens and John W. Loftus have attacked the Bible from cover to cover with a passion that equals that of any preacher of the gospel. An example would be this statement from Loftus: "My contention is that there is not a single statement in the Bible that reveals a divine mind behind the human authors. Everything in it can be more credibly explained by the hypothesis that it's just the musings of an ancient, superstitious, barbaric people, period."[1]

While sweeping attacks like this may do some damage to the kingdom (and our enemy will certainly use every method at his disposal), by far the more effective ploy is simply for Satan to make one little command seem out of touch with our real-world experience and let the trouble flow from there.

Solomon is the perfect example.

His marriage to the Egyptian pharaoh's daughter didn't require any grand renunciation of his faith in God. In fact, the day-to-day routine around the palace wouldn't have looked any different after the young woman arrived because Solomon gave her lodging elsewhere to keep from raising eyebrows. To the casual observer, it appeared as if nothing had changed, which is the goal of every gifted burglar.

But of course, something had changed.

The lock had been picked.

Satan had succeeded in convincing Solomon that one of God's most important commands was out of touch with his real-world experience.

And oh, the trouble it led to! One slight but necessary deviation from God's Word (as it would have been described by Solomon and his advisors) went largely unnoticed by the people, but was a harbinger of things to come. By the time Solomon's reign came to an end, countless compromises had been made and the kingdom was in a downward spiral.

A review of Solomon's life reveals that the majority of his violations of God's Word related to three very direct commands:

First, he broke the command God gave to all his people not to marry pagans. Deuteronomy 7:3–4 says, "You must not intermarry with them. Do not let your daughters and sons marry their sons and daughters, for they will lead your children away from me to worship other gods."

Second, he broke the command God gave to kings not to marry many wives. Deuteronomy 17:17 says, "The king must not take many wives for himself, because they will turn his heart away from the LORD."

And third, he broke the command God gave to kings not to accumulate great wealth. Deuteronomy 17:17 says, "And he must not accumulate large amounts of wealth in silver and gold for himself."

As I pointed out in chapter 1, there's zero chance that Solomon was unaware of these commands. His father, David, the man after God's own heart, took great pains to instruct him in the finer points of the Mosaic law. And just before he died, David drove the point home in a final message to his son: "Observe the require-ments of the LORD your God, and follow all his ways. Keep the decrees, commands, regulations, and laws written in the Law of Moses so that you will be successful in all you do and wherever you go" (1 Kings 2:3).

What we have here is a case not of ignorance or confusion or misinterpretation, but of Satan subtly and artfully manipulating Solomon's thinking to the point where he felt the commands of God seemed out of touch with his real-world experience.

CHECK YOUR LOCK

Clearly, Satan, the ultimate cat burglar, is still picking locks to this day. Churches are full of Christian men who've been suckered by Satan's reasoning, from the groom-to-be who decides to get a head start on the honeymoon, to the salesman who stretches the truth in order to make the sale, to the household accountant who fudges on his income tax. None of these behaviors are uncom-mon. Many would call them normal. What's more, they allow a man to keep a good standing in his church because, again, Satan is smart enough to quietly pick the lock rather than blowing up the door. But however quiet and socially acceptable these behav-iors may be, they still ultimately make a statement about how a man views God's commands.

Now would be a good time to check your own lock. Has Satan picked it? Has he convinced you to set aside one or more of God's commands in the name of expediency? If so, let me warn you of the consequences you will almost certainly face if you don't take immediate steps to reestablish strict biblical boundaries in your life. They are clearly seen in Solomon's life.

CONSEQUENCE #1: YOU WILL MAKE A FOOL OF YOURSELF

The subtitle of this book is *What You Can Learn from the Wisest Fool in the Bible*. Even after months of living with that title, I still have to tilt my head and squint when I read it. The notion of a "wise fool" just doesn't quite compute. Yet there can be no disputing that Solomon, the wisest man in the world, made an utter fool of himself.

Consider Exhibit A.

First Kings 11:5 says, "He [Solomon] followed Ashtoreth the goddess of the Sidonians, and Molech the detestable god of the Ammonites" (NIV). These were two of the pagan gods that Solomon's many wives worshipped. Verse 7 adds Chemosh, the god of the Moabites, to the list. And verse 8 suggests that there were other gods to boot.

If you're not familiar with these pagan gods, understand that they were the worst of the worst in terms of the practices of their adherents. Ashtoreth, for example, was the goddess of fertility, the female counterpart of Baal, and was worshipped with sex acts. Molech and Chemosh, who seem to have been related, had an insatiable thirst for blood, supposedly delighting when parents sacrificed their children (2 Kings 3:27).

That Solomon would allow the worship of these detestable false gods anywhere in the kingdom is terrible. That he would participate in that worship is unthinkable, but that's exactly what happened. In case you missed it, 1 Kings 11:5 says he "followed" these gods. He didn't just allow his wives to come toting their little figurines into the palace. He didn't just tolerate their behind-closed-doors rituals. No, he actually participated!

That in itself makes him a first-class, Grade-A fool, but even that's not all there is to say on the subject. One additional fact that is often overlooked stretches the limits of reason almost to the breaking point: Solomon worshipped the gods of nations he had conquered!

Think about that.

You've gone to war.

You've fought an enemy that prayed to its god for victory.

You've defeated that enemy and shown its god to be impotent.

And now you're going to bow down and worship that impotent, defeated god?

Really?

This kind of epic foolishness is what people eventually come to when they deem the Word of God to be out of touch and start making choices according to the feeling of the moment. This book would be a thousand pages thick if I took the time to relate the stories of Christian men who demonstrated mind-bending foolishness in their personal lives. One pastor I know was having an affair with two different women in his church at the same time! Another was storing nude pictures of his secret girlfriend on his laptop, which his teenage daughter decided to borrow one day when he was gone and hers went on the blink.

We hear stories like this and shake our heads. "Dumb, dumb, dumb," we say. But that's just it. These men are *not* dumb, any more than Solomon was. Many of them are sharp, educated guys with good heads on their shoulders.

Their problem is that their locks were picked.

Somehow, some way, Satan convinced them that a command of God was out of touch with real-world experience. Like Solomon, each made a seemingly small compromise that worked out well, which led to another and another and another. Before they knew it, they were neck deep in the kind of behavior they never dreamed they'd be capable of. And staring at a reputation so damaged it would take years to repair.

Right now, are you in danger of making a complete fool of yourself? Are you involved in some behavior that has escalated from risky to dangerous to unconscionable? Are you caught up in a relationship or activity that would be impossible to explain to your wife or your kids or your church family if it were to become known?

Whatever you do, don't tell yourself that you're smart enough to handle it and avoid trouble. If Solomon, the wisest man in the world, wasn't smart enough to handle it and avoid trouble, there's no reason why any of us should think we are.

CONSEQUENCE #2: YOU WILL LEAD OTHERS INTO SIN

It's ironic that when Solomon welcomed the Egyptian pharaoh's daughter into his life, he saw it as a great thing for the kingdom. Like a US president touting his signature piece of legislation, he would have been able to expound on the many ways the people were going to be blessed by the decision.

But history shows a different outcome.

Solomon's decision to marry an Egyptian princess was the first step down a long road toward disaster. For a while the nation prospered purely on the strength of Solomon's wisdom. But as the people saw him adding more and more foreign women to his harem, they began lowering their own standards, causing life in the kingdom to become increasingly pagan. Eventually, idolatry became as common in the villages as it was in the palace. No one can point to a day on the calendar when it happened, but there was a point at which the nation officially fell into full-scale spiritual decay.

Call it the "Yeast Effect." The idea comes from 1 Corinthians 5, where Paul addressed the sexual immorality that was occurring within the Corinthian church. Things had gotten so bad that a man was living openly with his stepmother. (Sounds like a modern-day reality show!) And the church leaders weren't dealing with the situation. They seemed to be proud of themselves for being able to tolerate such behavior without losing their spiritual cool. Paul basically told them they *needed* to lose their spiritual cool. He demanded that they call a meeting of the church and throw the man out if he refused to repent. His reasoning was well stated: "Don't you realize that this sin is like a little yeast that spreads through the whole batch of dough?" (1 Cor. 5:6).

Nothing spreads quite like sin.

The reason is revealed all the way back in Genesis 4. You'll remember that God had rejected Cain's offering and accepted his brother Abel's, which caused Cain to go into full sulk mode. I find it interesting that God did not try to comfort him or give him a pep talk, which is what most of us would have done. I, for one, would have patted Cain on the shoulder and said, "That's okay. Everybody makes mistakes. Just make sure you bring a better offering next time." Instead, God skipped the pep talk and the shoulder pat and issued a grave warning: "Sin is crouching at the door, eager to control you. But you must subdue it and be its master" (v. 7).

Picture it.

Sin is crouching at the door, eager to control you.

It crouches at the door of every heart—hungry, coiled, and ready to spring. It leaps from person to person like a brushfire on a windy day or, yes, a little yeast in a batch of dough. Just two chapters after God gave this warning to Cain, the entire population of the world was corrupt, except for Noah and his family. And not just a little corrupt. Genesis 6:5 says, "The LORD observed the extent of human wickedness on the earth, and he saw that everything they thought or imagined was consistently and totally evil."

Sin is crouching at the door . . .

. . . of your heart.

. . . of your home.

. . . of your church.

All it needs is a slight opening, which you will provide if you decide that one of God's commands is out of touch with your real-life experience and start doing things your own way. Like Solomon, you may be the first to break the command, but you won't be the last. People you love and care about will follow you into trouble.

CONSEQUENCE #3: YOU WILL MAKE AN ENEMY OF GOD

This is one of the most sobering aspects of Solomon's story. In the early chapters of 1 Kings, Solomon's relationship with God is a model for believers. The sweetest moment came when God offered to give Solomon anything he wanted. Solomon chose wisdom, which pleased God so much that he gave him wisdom and then threw in riches and fame for good measure. Things were going so well that in 1 Kings 5:4 Solomon said, "The LORD my God has given me peace on every side; I have no enemies, and all is well."

But look what happened just six chapters later.

First Kings 11:14 says, "Then the LORD raised up Hadad the Edomite, a member of Edom's royal family, to be Solomon's adversary."

And then just nine verses after that the Bible says, "God also raised up Rezon son of Eliada as Solomon's adversary" (v. 23).

The surprising thing here is not that Solomon faced adversaries. Israel was a major player on the world stage. There were jealousies and grudges among nations then just as there are today. What's stunning is that God himself raised up these leaders, empowering them to give Solomon trouble.

It's inevitable that we will have enemies in life, but you don't want to make an enemy of God. When God becomes your enemy, big trouble is in your future. Think about the flood God sent because he was disgusted with the depravity of mankind. Picture Sodom and Gomorrah being reduced to ashes by a shower of fire and brimstone. Consider the ten plagues God sent upon Pharaoh and the Egyptians. Imagine the whole Egyptian army being swallowed up in the waters of the Red Sea.

The Bible is full of frightening examples of God's wrath, and not all of it was directed at pagans. God allowed his own people to be defeated in battle and taken into captivity because of their unfaithfulness. And individuals like Samson, Jonah, and Solomon suffered terribly because of their disobedience.

This is something we probably don't think about enough today. When trouble comes into our lives we become philosophers. In between our whines and complaints, we speak of life in a fallen world and remind ourselves that Jesus promised we would have tribulation. We comfort ourselves by thinking about other people who've had our problems and worse. But what we should do is immediately check our behavior to see if we've given God any reason to oppose us.

I'm convinced that there are a lot of Christians who are praying to an angry God for deliverance. They're pleading with him to give them some relief, without realizing that the trouble they're facing is his response to their disobedience. People wonder why their prayers aren't answered. I suspect a good many are rejected because the person praying has unconfessed sin in his life of which he needs to repent.

BEEF UP SECURITY

If your lock has been picked, now is the time to relock it and add more layers of security. Even if the consequences mentioned above haven't hit home yet, it's only a matter of time before they do. Remember, Solomon's kingdom wasn't immediately thrown into chaos when he first began disobeying God. Things continued to go smoothly for a while. But if he'd listened carefully he could have heard the clock ticking in the background. Can you?

Here are three suggestions that will help you get back on track and beef up security for the future.

SUGGESTION #1: EVALUATE AND ADJUST YOUR PRIORITIES

There was a time when Solomon's priorities were few and simple. He wanted to serve God and his people well. That's why, when God offered to give him anything he wanted, he chose wisdom rather than fame and riches. But it wasn't long before other priorities found their way onto his list. He started obsessing over his image on the world stage, his personal comforts, and his many building projects (which I'll talk about in the next chapter). Before long, his priorities had become very muddled. What was once a very simple and happy life had become very complicated.

I've counseled a lot of seduced men over the last few decades, and I can tell you that muddled priorities are a common problem among them. It's not so much that they want *bad* things. It's more that they want too many things. Satan doesn't try to get you to forsake your good priorities. He just encourages you to mix in a few lesser priorities that will compete with those good priorities.

Most guys don't even realize how muddled their priorities are. Like Solomon, they see themselves as simply meeting the demands of everyday life. They work too many hours and rationalize it by saying, "This is what I have to do to get ahead." They settle for less than total honesty in order to cop a big commission and rationalize it by saying, "This is how the system works." Their wives and children (and perhaps many other people) can see how muddled their priorities are, but they don't see it themselves.

I find it interesting that at the end of Ecclesiastes, after telling his long, sad story, Solomon came full circle to affirm the simple priorities he once had as a young man. He said, "That's the whole story. Here now is my final conclusion: Fear God and obey his commands, for this is everyone's duty" (Eccl. 12:13). The other priorities that had worked their way into his life and distracted and occupied him for so many years were judged to be, in his words, "completely meaningless" (Eccl. 12:8). I'm guessing that every man who ever reads these words will have a few priorities in his life that are completely meaningless and need to be jettisoned.

That's why we need to periodically evaluate our priorities. If you don't know where to start, try keeping a log of how you spend your time. Then keep another one that tracks how you spend your money. Your time and your money are great truth-tellers. They always spill the beans about what's really going on in your heart. Then, at some point, you may want to have a heartfelt conversation with the people closest to you—your wife and/or children. Maybe your best friend or your boss. Ask them if they've noticed negative changes in you over the years. And don't get mad if they say yes. Imagine how much better off Solomon and the people of Israel might have been if someone who loved him had been honest enough to confront him about the changes they were seeing in his priorities.

SUGGESTION #2: EVALUATE AND ADJUST YOUR INFLUENCES

All heads of state have teams of advisors. Solomon's are listed in 1 Kings 4. You could call them his cabinet officials. In particular, it says that "Zabud son of Nathan, a priest, was a trusted adviser to the king" (v. 5).

These men failed Solomon.

They may have been loyal. They may have been supportive.

They may have been hard workers. They may have been somewhat spiritual. (Notice that Zabud was a priest.) But when Solomon started drifting off track, they didn't confront him and try to pull him back in line with God's Word. In fact, the greater likelihood is that they encouraged him to make shrewd political decisions that gave him status on the world stage but put him at odds with God.

Satan understands the power of influence one person can have over another. He tapped into it all the way back in the garden of Eden, sucking Eve into his clutches with a delectable temptation and then letting her bring Adam along all by herself. It didn't take her long to get the job done.

Guys have always been easy to influence. Women have always been able to wrap us around their little fingers. But sometimes I think the greater weakness we have is for our guy friends. Even if a friend has a long history of embarrassing failures, we will still listen to his advice because of a long history together. "We go way back" or "He's always had my back" are common statements guys use to justify their loyalty to questionable influences.

How many times have you read about a professional athlete getting into trouble during the off-season? Reports about altercations in bars and strip clubs have become standard fare on the sports page. Almost all of those articles speak of the high-profile athlete being out with friends, usually from the old neighborhood. He knows he's a public figure and could do great damage to his reputation and career. Team officials have warned him to keep his nose clean. He's seen his peers get in trouble doing the very same thing. But somehow being with old friends lessens the sense of danger.

One surefire way to beef up security and seduce-proof your life is to surround yourself with people who themselves have proven difficult for Satan to seduce.

SUGGESTION #3: EVALUATE AND ADJUST YOUR DIRECTION

Several years ago John Trent wrote a book called *The 2 Degree Difference*. In that book he contends that the best way to fix a big problem is by making small changes. Our tendency is to do the opposite. We assume that the only way to fix a big problem is by taking extreme measures. But extreme measures are often unsustainable over the long haul. (Been on a crash diet lately? Have a set of expensive weights collecting dust in your garage?) The better approach is simply to make a small change and stick with it. Adjust your direction by two degrees and you'll be in an entirely different place a year down the road. It's a great thought that I'm sure has helped a lot of people.

Unfortunately, the two-degree difference also works in reverse.

If your life is on track and you veer off by only two degrees, you'll be in an entirely different place a year down the road. Solomon is the poster boy for this truth. His life is a striking example of a man drifting ever so slightly off track. Starting in 1 Kings 3 and continuing through 1 Kings 11, we see the gap between where he was and where God wanted him to be growing gradually wider and wider.

The way to keep this from happening is by constantly evaluating your direction.

Yesterday I met a man who leads an international prayer ministry. He travels far and wide forty-plus weeks a year to help churches deepen their prayer lives. The question that immediately came to my mind concerned his marriage: How does he keep his marriage strong when he's gone so much?

The man has a deal with his wife. Once a year on a preselected date, they sit down together and she gets to evaluate their marriage. Notice, I said *she* gets to evaluate their marriage. His stated goal is to make every year of their marriage the best yet in *her* opinion. If she feels that he failed to accomplish that goal, then he asks her to explain where he failed and he makes adjustments. And here's the kicker. Only twice in over thirty years has he failed to accomplish his goal. That would be an admirable record even for a man who is home all the time! Clearly, those annual evaluations have helped keep him on track.

Imagine if Solomon had sat down once a year to evaluate his obedience to God's Word and then made immediate adjustments to get back on track. No doubt we would be reading a very different story in 1 Kings. It's hard for Satan to seduce a man who is constantly evaluating the direction of his life.

Mahatma Gandhi once spoke to an assembly of the House of Commons in England, which was, because of the circumstances of the time, a naturally hostile audience. He spoke for two hours without a single note and received a thunderous standing ovation when he finished. After the speech, reporters asked Gandhi's secretary, Mahadev Desai, how Gandhi was able to speak to a hostile audience so persuasively for so long without notes. Desai's answer is worth thinking about: "What Gandhi thinks, what he feels, what he says, and what he does are all the same. He does not need notes. . . . You and I, we think one thing, feel another, say a third, and do a fourth, so we need notes and files to keep track."[2]

Of course we would disagree with Gandhi's theology, but the consistency of his life would far exceed that of many believers. Certainly it exceeds what we see in Solomon, who was called by God and challenged by his father, David, to live in a straight line but ended up wandering all over the map.

That wandering started, as it always does for believers, with the thought that one of God's commands was a bit too restrictive, a little out of touch with real-life experience. As thoughts go, it's far from the ugliest. But make no mistake. It was conceived in the darkest corner of the pit of hell and has served our enemy well, enabling him to pick the lock on many a good man's heart.

Proverbs 4:23 says, "Guard your heart above all else, for it determines the course of your life." Now would be a good time to beef up security.

WAKE-UP CALL № 3

YOU KNOW YOU'RE BEING SEDUCED WHEN YOUR GLORY IS MORE IMPORTANT TO YOU THAN GOD'S GLORY

MANY PEOPLE WHO READ THIS BOOK WILL NOT BE OLD ENOUGH TO remember the televangelist scandals of the 1980s. Names like Jim and Tammy Faye Bakker, Jessica Hahn, Marvin Gorman, Debra Murphree, and Jimmy Swaggart may ring a faint bell with the under-forty crowd, but the details of their notoriety will likely be fuzzy. However, those of us who are over forty and make our livings in ministry will never forget those dark and painful days.

I was in my thirties at the time. Night after night on the news we had to suffer through yet another episode of what could have been called "Preachers Gone Wild." Lavish lifestyles, misappropriation of donations, hush-money payoffs, sexual encounters with secretaries and prostitutes, and failed lie detector tests were all a part of the story. I remember one lady in the church where I was preaching at the time who was a big Jimmy Swaggart supporter. I think she must have had every Jimmy Swaggart pamphlet, Bible, and record album in print. So when it was reported that Mr. Swaggart had met a prostitute at a New Orleans motel, she shook her fist and raged at the lying media. How dare they slander such a good man? Later, when it became known that there were pictures verifying the rendezvous (and when Swaggart tearfully fessed up and took a leave of absence from his ministry), the poor lady stopped raging at the media and took to her sick bed. Literally. I went to see her and she was as weak and listless as someone with a deadly disease.

The Jim Bakker quagmire was equally as sordid. His PTL Club (Praise the Lord Club) was so geared toward excess that detractors often quipped that "PTL" stood for "Pass the Loot." A reporter from the *Charlotte Observer* investigated the organization and published a series of articles that blew the lid off of PTL's irregular accounting practices, including the accusation that Bakker's people, with his blessing, kept two completely different sets of books to hide their shenanigans. And who could forget the church secretary that Bakker slept with? Jessica Hahn (who later posed for *Playboy*) received a hush-money payment of $279,000 that came from PTL funds, an expenditure I'm sure the ministry's financial supporters would never have envisioned or approved. Ms. Hahn said she was drugged and raped, while Bakker said the sex was consensual. Some people believed her while others believed him. The one thing everyone agreed on was that the ministry had long since gone off the rails and become desperately dysfunctional and diabolically dishonest. So dysfunctional that Bakker became the butt of a thousand jokes and so dishonest that he ended up in prison.

I am not a psychologist. Nor have I ever spoken with either Jimmy Swaggart or Jim Bakker. I suspect a team of shrinks could spend years burrowing down into the layers of issues that caused them to do what they did. But there is one thing I do know: they were seduced. Assuming there was a time when they were a couple of normal, down-to-earth, level-headed, God-fearing guys, there came a point at which they were anything but. It likely didn't happen overnight, but gradually. At some point *their* glory was becoming more important to them than God's glory.

Perhaps it was the TV thing, always having their hair and makeup just right and a camera in their faces and an adoring studio audience hanging on their every word. Maybe it was the letters they received from all over creation, seeking their counsel and begging for their prayers as if *their* prayers somehow carried more weight than anyone else's. Or maybe it was the donations that came pouring, Niagara-like, into their coffers. Most churches and ministries scratch and claw to pay their bills, but the PTL Club in particular was swimming in cash. I don't think there are very many people who could experience so much worldly success without having some ego issues.

Solomon sure couldn't.

In 1 Kings 3, at the very beginning of his reign, Solomon was the picture of humility. Read carefully what he said when God offered to give him anything he wanted:

> "You showed faithful love to your servant my father, David, because he was honest and true and faithful to you. And you have continued your faithful love to him today by giving him a son to sit on his throne.
>
> "Now, O LORD my God, you have made me king instead of my father, David, but I am like a little child who doesn't know his way around. And here I am in the midst of your own chosen people, a nation so great and numerous they cannot be counted! Give me an understanding heart so that I can govern your people well and know the difference between right and wrong. For who by himself is able to govern this great people of yours?" (vv. 6–9)

There may be no better picture of humility in the entire Bible. Solomon acknowledged that he was on the throne only because God put him there. And he admitted that he was not up to the task of governing such a great nation. He said, "I am like a little child who doesn't know his way around" and "who by himself is able to govern this great people of yours?" Notice those last words: "this great people of *yours*." Solomon understood that these were God's people, not his, and that he was simply being called upon to serve.

At this point we want to stand up and applaud Solomon. How unique is it (especially for people in our generation) to see a national leader who isn't full of himself, who doesn't think he has all the answers, and who understands who's really in charge?

Sadly, it wasn't long before Solomon's ego began to grow.

EGO ON STEROIDS

The steroid era of Major League Baseball has ended, but the memories it gave us won't be going away any time soon. As a Cardinals fan, I will never forget the summer of 1998. Mark McGwire and Sammy Sosa locked horns in a season-long game of home run derby. Night after night on ESPN we watched those guys hit blast after blast. Their soaring fly balls became tiny white specks against the night sky before crashing into the second or third deck. The whole country was caught up in the chase for Roger Maris's record.

I'll never forget the first time I saw pictures of several major league players that showed what they looked like both before and after they allegedly started taking steroids. Sammy Sosa and Barry Bonds didn't even resemble their former selves. Obviously, a lot of us "inflate" as we get older. But this was different. This wasn't a case of an aging athlete developing love handles or a paunch. This was a case of skinny speedsters becoming hulking power hitters. This was a case not just of biceps becoming huge, but of hat sizes and shoe sizes increasing dramatically. The comparison pictures were stunning.

And so it was with Solomon's ego. In 1 Kings 3 his ego is well contained. Healthy and strong to be sure, but certainly not out of control. However, over the next seven chapters it swells and morphs into a monstrosity. Where you see it so vividly is in his prayer and speech at the dedication of the temple. Six times he says the words "I have built" (1 Kings 8:13, 20, 27, 43, 44, 48).

That fact has special meaning for me because back in 2003 Poinciana Christian Church completed the construction of a new building. I was the lead minister throughout the whole project, from the purchase of the property to the laying of the carpet. I attended a slew of meetings and spent countless hours on site getting my hands dirty. But if I had stood up at the dedication service and talked about the building "I have built," I imagine my elders would have charged the stage and physically dragged me out of the pulpit, as well they should have.

I can't imagine words more ego-bloated than "I have built." They completely disregard the architects, construction managers, financial donors, physical laborers, inspectors, and skilled craftsmen without which no building project could ever be completed.

I've never heard a baseball player say, "I won the World Series!"

I've never heard a congressman say, "I passed the law!"

I've never heard a husband say, "I had a baby!"

Mark it down. When the word *I* starts replacing the word *we* in your speech, something ugly is happening in your heart. Your ego is swelling.

Other indications of Solomon's inflating ego can be seen in

the book of Ecclesiastes. Here's one example: "So I became greater than all who had lived in Jerusalem before me, and my wisdom never failed me. Anything I wanted, I would take. I denied myself no pleasure. I even found great pleasure in hard work, a reward for all my labors" (Eccl. 2:9–10).

That first phrase stands as a monument to arrogance, especially when you stop to think about some of the people who had lived in Jerusalem before Solomon (like his own father, David). But the second phrase may be even worse. Notice he said, "and my wisdom never failed me." Not "the wisdom God gave me never failed me," but "*my* wisdom never failed me."

In their book *Lead Like Jesus*, Ken Blanchard and Phil Hodges say that the word *ego* stands for "Edge God Out."[1] Clever, but oh how true. In Solomon's life, God's glory was edged out by his own. If you're looking for a single reason why Solomon's life got so completely out of whack, you need look no further than this.

SIDE EFFECTS

There are people who claim that having a big ego is a key to success in life. The logic goes something like this: People with big egos perceive themselves in such positive terms that they find it almost impossible to picture themselves failing, which, if you believe in the power of positive thinking, actually increases their chances of succeeding. They see themselves as being smarter and more capable than everyone else, and they behave accordingly. They tend to take charge and accept risks that other people would shy away from. And, not to be overlooked, their overpowering aura often intimidates potential adversaries. The result is that people with big egos often win their battles without having to fire a shot.

I don't have an argument with any of that. Anybody can see that wimpy, insecure people are seldom high achievers. But just as athletes get a performance boost from steroids, they also have to deal with the side effects. Allow me to mention some of the negative side effects that people with steroid-injected egos will encounter.

SIDE EFFECT #1: A DISCONNECTION FROM REALITY

A few years ago I had one of the most bizarre conversations of my life. A woman I had never met made an appointment to see me about a personal matter. I had no clue what to expect. It turned out that she was a college professor who attended a church not far from ours. She said, "I want to tell you about something my preacher did, and then I want you to tell me if it's normal . . . if it's the kind of thing preachers typically do."

I couldn't imagine what was coming.

She said, "My preacher asked me if I could pull some strings at the university where I teach and help get him an honorary doctor's degree. He only has a bachelor's, but he says that he knows as much as anyone who has a doctorate, and that his life's work is equal to that of many who have doctorates. He said that it would draw more people to our church if he could list himself as Dr. So-and-so on our promotional literature."

I thought about asking if she was kidding, but I could tell she wasn't.

I said, "I think I already know the answer to this question, but why doesn't he just do the work and earn himself a doctorate?"

She smiled and said, "I asked him the same thing. He said that he had more important work to do and, besides, he doubted that he would learn much that he didn't already know, which would make the process a waste of time." Then she added, "So, am I right to be offended by this? Or is this the kind of thing preachers do?"

My answer was that it is definitely not the kind of thing

preachers do. It's the kind of thing egomaniacs do, regardless of their profession. I mean, seriously, what planet did this preacher think he was living on? I don't know of a single accredited university anywhere in the world that hands out free doctorate degrees to anyone who thinks he deserves one.

This is the kind of thing people do when their egos are on steroids. They think so highly of themselves that they lose all perspective on reality, causing their words and actions to often fall outside the boundaries of real-world decorum.

Solomon, for example, ended up with seven hundred wives and three hundred concubines. On what planet is that normal? Think of the multiplicity of difficult personalities and annoying habits. Picture the cat fights that must have gone down in the women's quarters as Solomon's more domineering wives tried to assert themselves. Imagine the whining that must have filled the air as first one woman and then another felt mistreated or neglected. And picture Solomon getting dragged into fracas after fracas as a mediator or peacemaker. He was, after all, the guy in charge and, by his own admission, the one whose wisdom never failed.

Obviously, this was an absurd situation that only a person who had lost touch with reality would allow to develop. I mean, seriously, wouldn't you think that somewhere along the line, maybe at wife number nine or ten, a person in touch with reality might have said, "Wait a minute! This situation is getting out of control. Maybe we ought to back up and take another look at how we're doing things"? Even the most dedicated of ladies' men would surely call time-out and question the wisdom of collecting wives like some guys collect baseball cards.

But that's the thing about big-ego people. They almost never back up and take another look at their actions. Why should they? They're convinced that everything they do is right. It never occurs to them that they might be on the wrong track. They're so infatuated with themselves that they can see nothing but that beautiful image in the mirror.

SIDE EFFECT #2: INSENSITIVITY TO THE PROBLEMS AND NEEDS OF OTHERS

Solomon became very insensitive as his ego and ambitions grew. Check out 1 Kings 9:15: "This is the account of the forced labor that King Solomon conscripted to build the Lord's Temple, the royal palace, the supporting terraces, the wall of Jerusalem, and the cities of Hazor, Megiddo, and Gezer."

Forced labor.

We have a word for that: slavery.

There is some confusion as to who these slaves were. Later in the chapter we're told they were non-Israelites who were living in the land. However, in an apparent contradiction, 1 Kings 5:13 says, "King Solomon conscripted a labor force of 30,000 men from all Israel." So which is it? Did this conscripted labor force include Israelites or not? It appears that those slaves who were conscripted to serve permanently were not Israelites, but those who were given time off were Israelites (5:14).

Here's the point. This forced labor, even with the built-in time off, was considered oppressive and was bitterly resented by the people. We know this because after Solomon's death, representatives of the northern tribes of Israel said to Solomon's son, Rehoboam: "Your father was a hard master . . . Lighten the harsh labor demands and heavy taxes that your father imposed on us. Then we will be your loyal subjects" (1 Kings 12:4).

In typical big-ego fashion, Solomon was so obsessed with his building projects, so determined to see them completed, so anxious to bask in their magnificent glory, that he was willing to overwork and overtax his people.

Have you ever worked for a person who was in love with himself? If so, you know that he is only concerned with his own problems and needs. The only reason why he would address your problems and needs is if they somehow tie into his. Like the elder I once worked for who said to his fellow elders, "I guess we should give the staff a little raise. We might look bad if we don't."

I'm sure you can just imagine how robust the staff's morale was.

As I see it, this is one of the most visible effects of having a big ego. Your insensitivity will cause people not to like or respect you. Words like *arrogant, pompous, stuck-up,* and *prima donna* will be used to describe you. Your employees will nod and listen to what you say (because they have to) and then roll their eyes and complain as soon as you turn your back. Solomon may have looked magnificent perched on the throne in his royal robes, but outside the palace walls his people were bellyaching big time.

SIDE EFFECT #3: A DIMINISHING VIEW OF GOD

In John 3 we find John the Baptist running a robust baptizing ministry at a place called Aenon. He could have tried to parlay that success into a larger role in God's plan. He might have said, "Look at all these people coming to me for baptism. Surely I've earned a promotion. Maybe Jesus will allow me to work alongside him as a full and equal partner." Instead, in a true spirit of humility, John said of Jesus, "He must become greater and greater, and I must become less and less" (v. 30).

With Solomon it was just the opposite.

As his ego grew he became less concerned about God's glory and more concerned about his own. Nowhere is this seen more vividly than in 1 Kings 6:37–7:1: "The foundation of the temple of the LORD was laid in the fourth year, in the month of Ziv. In the eleventh year in the month of Bul, the eighth month, the temple was finished in all its details according to its specifications. He had spent seven years building it. It took Solomon thirteen years, however, to complete the construction of his palace" (NIV).

In an odd confluence of circumstances, my wife and I ended up building a new house at the same time Poinciana Christian Church's new church building was under construction. Let me tell you: we were sick to death of sawdust and drywall dust and paint smells. On the other hand, it sure was nice to be moving into new digs both at work and at home. Our house ended up costing less than one-tenth of what our church building cost, and it took much less time to build. Compare that to Solomon's palace. We don't have a move-in price, but we know it took him almost twice as long to build as it did to build the temple.

Imagine if your preacher lived in a house that was twice the size and cost of the church building where you worship. In my case, I would be living in a forty-thousand-square-foot home that cost $3.4 million. I would be able to fit about twenty of my church members' homes inside my own. And then imagine that your preacher didn't see anything wrong with such an arrangement!

Here's a simple and undeniable fact: the larger a man's ego gets, the less he cares about God's glory. He may still go to church and be involved in religious activities. (Solomon never stopped going through the motions of worship.) But at some point his religious activities cease to be about God's glory and become, instead, a vehicle for self-promotion. Jesus warned his disciples about this when he said, "And when you pray, do not be like the hypocrites, for they love to pray standing in the synagogues and on the street corners to be seen by others" (Matt. 6:5 NIV).

Notice the phrase "they love to pray." Egomaniacs are often the most overtly religious people in the church. They love to pray. They love to teach. They love to do anything that puts them in the spotlight. What they don't love is God. At least not as much as they love themselves.

THE STEROID-FREE EGO

So how are you doing in the ego department?

If you saw yourself in any of the preceding paragraphs, it's definitely time for you to get off the steroids and allow some ego shrinkage to take place.

Don't worry. It won't hurt you a bit.

Since Major League Baseball instituted stricter policies against performance-enhancing drugs, the stats have shrunk. No longer are we seeing muscle-bound hulks producing sixty-home-run seasons. You might think this would produce a less attractive game, but that's not true. As the game has gotten cleaner there's been no drop-off in excitement.

Likewise, if you start embracing humility, you won't have to worry about suddenly losing your mojo. Some of the most success-ful people in history were known for their humility. Try googling the words "humble people in history." I did, and several lists came up. On those lists were St. Francis of Assisi, Leonardo DaVinci, Abraham Lincoln, Albert Einstein, Gandhi, Mother Teresa, and a host of other people who have earned the world's respect.

But what exactly does it mean to embrace humility?

First, it means admitting you're not a slave to your ego. Most big-ego people, when challenged about their arrogance, trot out the ever-popular, catch-all excuse that spiritually lazy people have been falling back on for eons: "This is just the way God made me." Or "This is just the way I'm wired." That answer melts like the Wicked Witch of the West in the light of God's Word. Again and again the Bible tells us to humble ourselves, to walk humbly, and to serve humbly, indicating that humility is not a spiritual gift that some people have and other people don't. It's a choice.

Second, embracing humility means submitting to the author-ity of God. Why? Because all arrogance is ultimately defiance against God. It plays itself out horizontally in our careers and relationships, as I explained earlier. But if you drill down into the core of the problem, what you always find is a heart perched on the throne that rightfully belongs to God. Again, *ego* stands for "Edging God Out." Or "Edging God Off" his throne. This is why Peter said, "Humble yourselves *under* the mighty power of God" (1 Peter 5:6, author's emphasis).

Finally, embracing humility means abandoning your quest for position. Remember when Mrs. Zebedee approached Jesus and requested that her two sons, James and John, be allowed to sit at his right hand in heaven? I picture Jesus sighing internally so as not to embarrass her, taking a deep breath, and then patiently explaining what every Christian needs to know and remember: In his kingdom greatness is not achieved by jockeying for position. It is, in fact, achieved when you *stop* jockeying for position. Specifically, Jesus said that whoever wants to be first must become a slave (Matt. 20:27).

In practical terms, abandoning your quest for position means you're not always trying to edge your way toward the spotlight. It means you're willing to serve even when you know in advance you're not going to get any credit. It means you don't always have to have your way, that you recognize other people can have good ideas too (and that you can have bad ones). It means you don't sulk or pout or pursue paybacks when you don't get your way. It means you take responsibility for your mistakes instead of trying to funnel blame off onto others. Most of all, it means yielding your will to God's.

I understand that embracing humility can be hard for people who have reaped the worldly benefits that having a big ego can bring. Once you get your fanny planted on that throne, climbing down off of it can be hard. But the alternative is to live your life disconnected from reality, with people genuinely not liking you, and with God as your opponent rather than your friend. I'll be talking about this in depth in chapter 9. For now, let me just plant the seed. James 4:6 gives us eight words that should make spotlight seekers everywhere stop and think: "God opposes the proud but favors the humble."

Think about that.

As if all the other negative side effects of a pumped-up ego aren't bad enough, God will begin actively opposing you. How much more difficult will that make your life? How many more failures and disappointments will you have if God is working against you? How might he empower your enemies and opponents? How might he undermine your dreams? Sure, you'll have some successes. If nothing else, your bloated ego will intimidate the insecure, causing them to scamper out of your way. But by whose definition is that true success? It's like being the overgrown bully on the playground. You may get your way, but not for any of the right reasons.

Life brings enough opponents across your path already. There's no need to turn God into one too.

My favorite movie is *The Wizard of Oz*. Not very macho, but if you're paying attention there's a sermon illustration about every five minutes from start to finish (and little else matters to us preachers).

Take the Wizard himself.

He is the Great and Powerful Oz, a legend throughout Munchkinland, the beating heart of the Emerald City. People—or rather, munchkins—bow and scrape and tremble in his presence. No one dares to question his wisdom or disobey one of his commands. But in the end he is exposed. It turns out that he is just a man, and a rather bumbling one at that. One of my favorite lines comes when his cover is blown: "Pay no attention to that man behind the curtain!"

Solomon was very Oz-like. He, too, was a legend throughout the known world. Accomplished people traveled from far and wide to bow and scrape in his presence. Even a bare morsel of the king's wisdom was treated like a nugget of pure gold. World leaders begged for his friendship, and the line of women outside his bedroom door stretched around the block. The Great and Powerful Solomon becoming drunk on his own worldly success is about as surprising as the New England Patriots having a winning record. But in the end he, too, was exposed. With failures piled higher than the walls of his palace, it finally became apparent that all along he had just been a man hiding behind a curtain, and a rather bumbling one at that. So bumbling that even the favor of almighty God couldn't save him from himself.

Perhaps in your own personal Munchkinland you have become the Great and Powerful Mike. Or the Great and Powerful Joe. Or the Great and Powerful Tom. Maybe you've fumed and blustered your way to some worldly success and have come to think of yourself as better than everybody else. And maybe you've won enough accolades and trophies and promotions to make others believe it too.

Don't kid yourself. You're just a man, and a rather bumbling one at that.

We all are.

WAKE-UP CALL №4

YOU KNOW YOU'RE BEING SEDUCED WHEN YOU'RE MORE INFLUENCED BY ENTICEMENTS THAN WARNINGS

I WAS PLAYING GOLF WITH MY BUDDY DAVID BAKER. I HAD KNOCKED my ball into a knee-deep patch of weeds (which isn't unusual for me) and, figuring I'd never be able to find it, was digging another one out of my bag. David, feeling sorry for me because it was about the fourth ball I'd lost that afternoon (which also isn't unusual for me), was making a half-hearted effort to look for it, consoling me as he kicked around the edge of the weeds.

Suddenly, he yelped and hotfooted it toward the cart. "Rattler!" he said.

I spun around. "Where?"

"Right there in the weeds. Didn't you hear it?"

"No," I said. "Are you sure?"

"Yes, I am."

I listened. "I don't hear anything."

"He's right there in the edge of the weeds."

I looked. "I don't see anything."

David picked up a stick and tossed it into the weeds from about eight feet away, the very picture of courage.

51

We listened.

Nothing.

I said, "Are you sure there's a rattler in there?"

"I promise you there's a rattler in there. I heard him rattling plain as day."

We never did see the rascal, but I trust my friend. If he says there was a rattler, there was a rattler. What struck me about the incident was the amazing power of that little rattling sound, which is the snake's way of warning you to back off. Talk about getting someone's attention. I doubt that David would have moved more quickly if someone had dropped a lit firecracker down his pants.

It's a shame we don't treat all warnings that way.

One day my wife, Marilyn, and I were sitting at a traffic light near the Mall at Millennia in Orlando. If you've been there, you know that area is the traffic equivalent of a hive of bees in full swarm. I was first in line in the far left of three lanes. There were two cars to my right and about fifty lined up behind the three of us.

When the light turned green, I happened to be fiddling with the radio and was slow to react. The driver on my immediate right was apparently antsy and stomped down hard on the gas, vaulting his vehicle forward. He was about fifteen feet from his starting point when an SUV came flying through the intersection from my left and hit him broadside. The impact created a thunderous explosion of glass and metal and sent the car rolling down the pavement. It turned over twice before settling right side up. My estimate is that the red-light runner was doing at least fifty-five or sixty.

There's no doubt he saw the light turn yellow and knew what it meant. But, like millions of people do every day, he ignored the warning and flattened the gas pedal. I never did hear if anyone died in that accident, but everyone was hauled to the hospital, and I'm sure, if nothing else, they were all scarred emotionally. I wasn't even involved, but for a long time after that I was skittish around intersections. For the next six months I got honked at again and again because I was so slow to step on the gas.

Sadly, a yellow traffic light is only one of many warnings that the otherwise intelligent male (OIM) has been known to ignore.

The OIM sees a wedding ring on an attractive woman's finger but flirts with her anyway.

The OIM takes a course in motorcycle safety, then turns right around and straps his helmet to the back of his bike before speeding off down the highway.

The OIM sees a sign that says Speed Limit 55 but drives 75 anyway.

The OIM hears a thousand public service announcements about the dangers of drinking and driving but still staggers out of the bar and slips behind the wheel of his car.

The OIM hears sermons and reads articles about the damaging effects of porn but still cruises the Internet's red-light district when his wife isn't around.

The OIM receives a Payment Past Due notice from his mortgage company but won't even think of canceling his NFL Sunday Ticket or missing his weekly golf game.

The OIM sees signs of discontent in his wife but continues to give more attention to his job than he does to her.

Guys, let's be honest. Virtually all the messes we get ourselves into are the result of us ignoring warnings. Not *missing* them but ignoring them, which, of course, is nothing new. Solomon was busy perfecting the art three thousand years ago.

His father, David, had drilled God's law into his head and warned him that he must obey that law if he wanted to be successful (1 Kings 2:1–3). And then God himself drove the point home:

> "If you walk before me in integrity of heart and uprightness, as David your father did, and do all I command and observe my

decrees and laws, I will establish your royal throne over Israel forever, as I promised David your father when I said, 'You shall never fail to have a man on the throne of Israel.'

"But if you or your sons turn away from me and do not observe the commands and decrees I have given you and go off to serve other gods and worship them, then I will cut off Israel from the land I have given them and will reject this temple I have consecrated for my Name. Israel will then become a byword and an object of ridicule among all peoples." (1 Kings 9:4–7 NIV)

That is an epic warning. I have no doubt that Solomon's head was nodding like a dashboard bobblehead on a bumpy road. *Yes, sir. I understand, sir. There will be no funny business as long as I'm on the throne, sir. You can count on me, sir!* And I'm sure he meant it.

But when a neighboring king showed up at the city gate with several cart loads of goodies and his smokin' hot virgin daughter, Solomon's resolve melted like a bowl of ice cream in a microwave. No, the hard drive between his ears wasn't suddenly wiped clean. He still remembered all those warnings; he just chose to ignore them.

If we're serious about staving off seduction and keeping ourselves pure and out of trouble, we've got to ask and answer a hard question.

WHAT MAKES US SO PRONE TO IGNORE WARNINGS?

I want to suggest four possible answers.

POSSIBLE ANSWER #1: WE HAVE A FLAWED VIEW OF OURSELVES

When professional sports franchises draft players, they're obviously looking for size and ability. Armies of scouts produce mountains of notes and countless hours of video that identify the players they feel offer the best combination of size, speed, skill, and intelligence. But the best franchises understand that there's more to having a successful draft than just choosing the most gifted players. The real key is choosing the most gifted players who are also coachable. If you follow sports, you know it's true. Every draft class contains gifted athletes who will never make it because they won't take instruction.

At its most basic level, a warning is an attempt to coach.

Take, for example, a recent public service announcement about the dangers of sun exposure. No doubt it caught my ear because I've had skin cancer surgery three times. I stopped what I was doing and gave the TV my full attention. The pictures and stats were sobering, the warning crystal clear. The narrator implored people to wear sunscreen and reapply often, in much the same way a coach would implore his players to wrap up on a tackle or get in front of a ground ball. It was coaching, pure and simple. Life coaching.

And like all coaching, it is being ignored by people who are not coachable.

Day after day I see construction workers toiling shirtless in the vicious Florida sun. I know golfers who'll hack for four hours without a hat or a single dollop of sunscreen. I go to the beach and see people sprawled on blankets, cooking themselves like a Thanksgiving turkey in grandma's oven. Am I supposed to believe that none of these people have ever heard of skin cancer? Of course they have. The problem is, they're not coachable.

Why?

Because they have a flawed view of themselves. They think they're smarter or more capable or more invincible than they really are. (After an entire chapter on ego, here we go again. Are you starting to get the idea that this is a big problem?)

Think about a person you've known who wouldn't take advice, perhaps a coworker or a family member. At some point you probably shook your head and said, "You can't tell him anything." You may not have used the word *arrogant*, but isn't that what was going through your mind? You realized that the person had put up a wall. He'd blocked you out because he didn't want to hear what you were saying or, more likely, didn't think he needed to hear it.

I find it interesting that the apostle Paul addressed the danger of arrogance when laying out the qualifications of elders in 1 Timothy 3. He said, "An elder must not be a new believer, because he might become proud, and the devil would cause him to fall" (v. 6).

Notice how Paul tied pride and moral failure together. He understood that arrogance leads a man to disregard rules and warnings and good advice and do things his own way.

Sounds like Solomon, doesn't it?

His arrogance drips off the pages of Ecclesiastes. Consider chapter 1, verse 16. Solomon said to himself, "Look, I am wiser than any of the kings who ruled in Jerusalem before me. I have greater wisdom and knowledge than any of them." This was true, of course, but that's not the point. Oftentimes, arrogant people are indeed extremely gifted. The point is that they put too much confidence in their giftedness. Solomon's giftedness became his excuse for doing things his own way. I can just hear his response when someone dared to question his bad decisions: *Why are you challenging me? Don't you know I'm the wisest person who ever lived?*

Think back over your own experience.

Think of a time when you really messed up.

Is it fair to say that you were too full of yourself? Too confident in your own ability? Too smug in the face of dissenting opinions? Too dismissive of the red flags that were flying in your face?

I have no doubt the answer is yes, because this sad fact has always been true: "Pride goes before destruction, and haughtiness before a fall" (Prov. 16:18).

POSSIBLE ANSWER #2: WE HAVE A FLAWED VIEW OF GOD

The following has happened to me at least twenty times. Every preacher or Christian counselor who reads the next paragraph will say, "Yup. Been there, done that."

I'm sitting in my office with a man who is involved in an illicit love affair. It might be a single guy who's in love with a married woman, or a married guy who's found that someone else's wife is more enticing than his own. At any rate, the person is all gaga over his paramour, but he knows he's swimming upstream. He knows the Bible says adultery is a no-no and that polite society frowns on such shenanigans. But, undaunted, he is determined to soldier on, arm in arm, with his new sweetheart. What's the basis of his defense? What's the line of reasoning with which he hopes to win the sympathy of your humble servant? The following assertion: "We know God loves us, and we just can't believe he would want us to be unhappy. In fact, we're convinced that our meeting was a 'God thing.' We really feel he brought us together."

Take a moment to gag if you need to.

I know it sounds absurd, but I'm telling you, people actually say things like this. And I'm convinced they believe what they're saying. How is that possible? How can otherwise intelligent people who've actually read the Bible come up with stuff like this?

Easy.

Satan is a master deceiver.

Ephesians 6:12 says, "For we are not fighting against flesh-and-blood enemies, but against evil rulers and authorities of the unseen world, against mighty powers in this dark world, and against evil spirits in the heavenly places."

Don't miss that word *mighty*.

Satan has *mighty* powers.

When an imperfect person with a major weakness meets a master deceiver with mighty powers, it's game over. Shut off the lights and lock the doors. That person will end up believing whatever Satan wants him to believe, no matter how ridiculous it seems to everyone else.

Think about Solomon.

The man actually came to believe it was a good idea to build altars to pagan gods on the Mount of Olives (1 Kings 11:7–8). Really, Solomon? Are you serious?

Imagine the mental gymnastics required to rationalize that little project. But he pulled it off. He did the floor exercise and stuck the landing. Because he had help: Satan whispering in his ear through every flip and cartwheel.

I used to be surprised at the crazy ideas otherwise intelligent people get into their heads, but not anymore.

And so it is that people feel it's safe to ignore God's warnings. With Satan's help, they convince themselves that God is not the cosmic party-pooper we preachers have made him out to be, that he is in fact all about chocolate candy and bunny slippers and group hugs, our big BFF in the sky. All he wants is for us to be happy.

Allow me to introduce you to the real God. He speaks about this business of warnings and how his people react to them in Malachi:

> "Listen to me and make up your minds to honor my name," says the Lord of Heaven's Armies, "or I will bring a terrible curse against you. I will curse even the blessings you receive. Indeed, I have already cursed them, because you have not taken my warning to heart. I will punish your descendants and

splatter your faces with the manure from your festival sacrifices, and I will throw you on the manure pile. Then at last you will know it was I who sent you this warning so that my covenant with the Levites can continue," says the LORD of Heaven's Armies. (Mal. 2:2–4)

I doubt you'll hear that passage read at church next Sunday morning, which, come to think of it, might be part of our problem.

POSSIBLE REASON #3: WE HAVE A FLAWED VIEW OF THE FUTURE

"It's easier to get forgiveness than permission."

The first time I heard somebody say that, I chuckled and thought, *That's clever.* So I added it to my repertoire of witty remarks. Since then I've said it many times myself, always with a touch of humor, but never about something really serious. (Unless you consider a momentary straying from my heart-healthy diet really serious.)

What concerns me is that countless men use this basic philosophy to justify their actions in matters that are extremely serious. Their thinking goes something like this: *I know I probably shouldn't do this, but I'm going to go ahead. If it blows up and gets messy, I can always apologize and make things right later.*

That train of thought is flawed on many levels, but one of the biggest problems I see with it is that it makes a faulty assumption. It assumes there will always be an opportunity to make things right later.

What if there isn't?

Remember the story of Ananias and Sapphira? In Acts 5 we're told that they sold a piece of property and gave a portion of the sale price to the apostles. The problem was that they lied to make themselves look more spiritual than they really were, telling the apostles they were giving the entire purchase price.

Imagine Ananias speaking to his wife as they were plotting this little deception: "Honey, I know what we're doing here is a little shady, but we're not hurting anybody. It's not like we're stealing or anything. And besides, if we get caught, we can always apologize. You know the apostles as well as I do. Those guys are all about grace and forgiveness. So don't worry, everything will be fine."

You may remember that they did indeed get caught and Ananias, who was undoubtedly the mastermind, was not given an opportunity to make things right. Peter chewed him out and then the Bible says, "As soon as Ananias heard these words, he fell to the floor and died" (Acts 5:5).

Who says there will always be an opportunity to make things right? I can think of four scenarios where that wouldn't be the case.

1. You could die before you have a chance to make things right.
2. The person you assume will forgive you might not.
3. Your actions could produce ripple effects that extend beyond your reach.
4. Your actions could cause damage that is impossible to repair.

Several years ago a man who had been imprisoned for drunk driving spoke at our church. Ordinarily, people don't go to prison for drunk driving, but this guy hit and killed a preschool-age child. Three things he said stuck with me. One, he estimated that before the accident he had heard thousands of warnings against drinking and driving and ignored them all. Two, he hit the child only a few blocks from his house, which meant he had to drive by that spot (and relive the memory) every time he went to and from home. And three, even if he gave a speech about the dangers of drinking and driving every day for the rest of his life, it would never make things right. Nothing would ever change the fact that he had killed a child.

Only a fool would ever say, "I can always make things right later." Solomon was right when he said, "Don't brag about tomorrow, since you don't know what the day will bring" (Prov. 27:1).

POSSIBLE REASON #4: WE HAVE A FLAWED VIEW OF SIN

As I am writing this chapter, the whole world is talking about a book called *Fifty Shades of Grey*, an erotic novel that continues to sell like crazy despite being panned by many literary critics. I've read a number of articles and blog entries that have attempted to explain the book's popularity. After all, there are a gazillion other erotic novels out there, apparently most of them better written (according to people who have read them and judge such things), that haven't sold nearly as well. The conclusion I've come to is that no one really understands why things like this happen. It's like trying to explain the Kardashians or Brussels sprouts.

The only thing I can think of that is more inexplicable than the popularity of *Fifty Shades of Grey* is the fact that it is being read and praised by a lot of Christians. I don't know exactly how many, but judging by the reader responses to some of the major Christian blogs and social media outlets, it's a fair amount.

I remember the day I signed on to Facebook and saw a post from a woman who was attending our church at the time. She said she had just finished reading *Fifty Shades of Grey* and couldn't wait to read the sequel. Just as disappointing was the fact that her post was punctuated with exclamation marks and smiley faces and two OMGs (an abbreviation for "Oh, my God!"). I thought it was an odd reaction for a woman who'd given birth to several kids. From her giggly, juvenile reaction you'd have thought she was just hearing about sex for the first time.

Sure enough, it wasn't long before other women were "liking" and commenting on her post. Then other Christian women who were outraged joined the fray. The resulting brouhaha was a thing to behold and might have been entertaining if it hadn't been so sad. The whole thing was a testimony to how lax our attitudes toward sin have become.

Now you might say, "But Mark, *Fifty Shades of Grey* is a women's book. We guys don't read stuff like that." You're right. Guys go straight for the pictures and videos. Estimates vary slightly, but most researchers agree that at least half of Christian men look at porn regularly. I've talked to a number of them over the years and far too many say the same thing: "What's the big deal? It doesn't change how I feel about my wife, and it adds a little spice to our marriage."

What's the big deal?

If ever a question spoke to the attitude of our generation toward sin, that one does. We shrug off sin as though it's just a little harmless fun. You know, boys will be boys. Everybody sows some wild oats, right?

Or, if we don't play the what's-the-big-deal card, we claim that the sin we're indulging in is actually necessary.

Take cohabitation, for example.

The Bible condemns sex outside of marriage, yet countless young couples, even after growing up in the church, choose to live together before tying the knot. If challenged, they often cut loose a pre-rationalized explanation of why such an arrangement is necessary.

"It helps us save money."

"We can't afford two house payments."

"It's only temporary until we can get some of our bills paid."

Naturally, nothing is ever said about the two of them simply wanting to play house and have sex before the wedding.

I've challenged Christian couples on their cozy premarital living arrangements, pointing out what the Bible says about sexual purity, only to have them look at me like I had stalks of celery sticking out of my ears. *Poor Mark, he just doesn't get it.* Of course they would never say it out loud, but it's clear that they think I'm making a mountain out of a molehill, especially when they go right on living together as if the conversation never happened.

Several years ago, a boy in South Florida found what appeared to be a colorful, nonvenomous scarlet kingsnake in his yard. He picked it up and started playing with it, showing it off to his friends. At one point he was holding it in front of his face, sticking his tongue out at it the way snakes do to us. When the snake struck and bit his cheek, he realized that it wasn't a scarlet kingsnake at all, but a deadly coral snake, which has similar coloring.

Millions of Christians routinely play with sins they think are harmless. Most of them get bitten sooner or later.

So let's review.

A flawed view of self.

A flawed view of God.

A flawed view of the future.

A flawed view of sin.

That's a lot of flawed thinking that makes us very easy to seduce.

What we need is some *clear* thinking.

THE TRUTH ABOUT GOD AND WARNINGS

God has been all about warnings since creation. The first thing he did after creating Adam, even before forming Eve out of Adam's rib, was to give Adam a warning. You'll find it on page 2 or 3 of your Bible: "The LORD God took the man and put him in the Garden of Eden to work it and take care of it. And the LORD God commanded the man, 'You are free to eat from any tree in the garden; but you must not eat from the tree of the knowledge of good and evil, for when you eat of it you will surely die'" (Gen. 2:15–17 NIV).

It's important that we break this warning down because it sets a pattern that is consistent throughout Scripture and even to this day. Remember, God does not change (Mal. 3:6). Notice three truths.

TRUTH #1: GOD'S WARNING TO ADAM WAS VERY SPECIFIC

He didn't just tell Adam that there was a tree that was off-limits. He actually named the tree and gave him its exact location (Gen. 3:3). He told him exactly what would happen if he chose to eat its fruit anyway. And, not to be overlooked, he made it clear to Adam exactly what fruit *was* okay to eat.

Thumb through the Bible and you'll see that all of God's warnings are specific, which is something we should appreciate because specificity is not all that common in our world. We're often forced to stagger and grope through the fog of ambiguity as we search for answers. For example, how many conversations like the following go down every day?

> **PARENT.** You can't do that.
> **TEENAGER.** Why?
> **PARENT.** Because I said so.
> **TEENAGER.** But why? There has to be a reason.
> **PARENT.** Because I don't think it's a good idea.
> **TEENAGER.** But you used to do it.
> **PARENT.** That's different.
> **TEENAGER.** Why is it different?

PARENT. Because times have changed.

TEENAGER. What do you mean?

PARENT. (exasperated) Look, when you get out on your own you can do what you want, but as long as you're living under my roof you'll do what I say.

Perhaps you can remember a day when you played the role of the teenager in that very conversation. If so, you probably remember how frustrated you felt. All you wanted was a straight answer, but all you got were cryptic responses.

God is never cryptic when giving a warning.

Solomon, of all people, knew this. First Kings 11:9–10 says, "The LORD was very angry with Solomon, for his heart had turned away from the LORD, the God of Israel, who had appeared to him twice. *He had warned Solomon specifically about worshiping other gods*, but Solomon did not listen to the LORD's command" (author's emphasis).

Why is God so specific? So when the time comes to deal with our disobedience, we can't plead ignorance and say we didn't understand. Solomon himself warned, "Don't excuse yourself by saying, 'Look, we didn't know.' For God understands all hearts, and he sees you. He who guards your soul knows you knew" (Prov. 24:12).

TRUTH #2: AFTER WARNING HIM, GOD CLOSELY MONITORED ADAM'S ACTIONS

The blush hadn't faded from Adam's cheeks before God was confronting him. "Have you eaten from the tree whose fruit I commanded you not to eat? (Gen. 3:11). Obviously, God already knew the answer to that question because he'd been watching. In Jeremiah 16:17 God said, "I am watching them closely, and I see every sin. They cannot hope to hide from me."

This is an aspect of God's character that I think we fail to appreciate. As I pointed out in chapter 1, privacy is second only to alcohol in its ability to make the taboo tempting. If we think we can do it without anyone seeing or knowing, we're much more likely to sin. But there is really no such thing as privacy. Even if no human is aware of what you're doing, God is.

Not long ago I heard a report on the news about the proliferation of security cameras. The expert being interviewed said that if you're in a city—any city, either outdoors or in a public building—there's about a 75 percent chance your actions are being recorded. The interviewer commented on how creepy that is. I thought, *So what's new?* There's been an "eye in the sky" on us since the beginning of time. The problem is that most people either refuse to believe it or forget about it.

TRUTH #3: GOD FOLLOWED THROUGH ON THE CONSEQUENCES HE PROMISED

When I was in college, a professor gave us a test that every person in the class failed. I mean, no one even came close to passing. As I recall, the highest grade (which wasn't mine) was somewhere in the fifties. The professor, in an act of considerable grace, said, "Since you all failed so miserably, there must have been something wrong with the test. I'm going to make up another one and give you guys another chance."

He did, and we all passed.

Similarly, God could have said to Adam and Eve, "Look, I realize this is all new to you. You'd never been tempted before and you had no idea how crafty Satan is. Maybe my expectations were a little too high. Tell you what, I'm going to wipe the slate clean and give you guys another chance."

But that's not what he did.

Rather, he followed through on his warning. These words to Adam are the most telling: "For you were made from dust, and to dust you will return" (Gen. 3:19).

God has yet to make his first empty threat. Yes, there are instances in Scripture where he changes his mind, but in each of those cases either intercession (Ex. 32:14) or repentance (Jonah 3:10) was involved, both of which are a part of his plan for dealing with mankind. But never—not once—has he ever given a hollow warning. The prophet Jeremiah had it right when he said, "But it is the LORD who did just as he planned. He has fulfilled promises of disaster he made long ago" (Lam. 2:17).

Taken together, these three truths add up to an inescapable conclusion: if you ignore God's warnings, you're not just flirting with disaster; you're holding out a ring and asking it to marry you.

Ask Solomon.

So what are we to do?

The best advice I can offer as I close this chapter comes, again, from Jeremiah. He said, "Why should we, mere humans, complain when we are punished for our sins? Instead, let us test and examine our ways" (Lam. 3:39–40).

WAKE-UP CALL №5

YOU KNOW YOU'RE BEING SEDUCED WHEN SIN MANAGEMENT SEEMS LIKE A BETTER CHOICE THAN REPENTANCE

MANAGEMENT IS HUGE THESE DAYS. WE'VE GOT A SLEW OF EXPERTS writing books and holding seminars on the best way to manage your business, your investments, your stress, your anger, your weight, your schedule, your income, your health, your volunteers, your reputation, and even your clutter.

Let me be clear about one thing: I am a big believer in good management.

Marilyn and I have a catchphrase we use often: "It's all about management." We say it when we can't get waited on in a restaurant because there aren't enough servers.

We say it when we can't get waited on even though there are more than enough servers.

We say it when we can't find a salesperson to help us with a major purchase.

We say it when we have a long wait at a doctor's office because they overbook appointments.

We say it when we walk into a retail store that is dirty and disorganized.

We say it when we encounter rude or unsympathetic employees.

In other words, we pretty much say it all the time.

So this chapter is no attack on management. Good management is something the world needs a lot more of. The reality, however, is that some things were never meant to be managed.

Imagine you're in the pest control business. A potential client calls and schedules an inspection. After giving the house the once-over and finding a serious cockroach problem, you recommend the standard "wipe those suckers out" treatment. But the homeowner says, "Oh no! I don't want to wipe them out. After all, they're God's creatures too. I just want to keep them away from our food and out of our bedroom."

Crazy, right?

But wait a minute!

Isn't that what people do with sin?

I'm talking about *millions* of people.

Instead of repenting . . . instead of exterminating, eliminating, or correcting their bad behavior, they try to manage it. They believe that if they can keep the behavior from getting out of hand, keep people from being hurt or offended, keep the status quo from being upset, keep the ugliness under wraps and out of sight, they can hang on to their sin and everything will be fine.

Solomon is a good example.

His headfirst plunge into the world of sin management came early in his reign. He'd just married the Egyptian pharaoh's pagan daughter and was taking a hit in the popularity polls. Tongues were wagging. The citizenry was offended by the presence of a pagan in the palace, which should have been a wake-up call for Solomon. It should have been his cue to repent and send the young woman packing. Instead, he chose to manage the situation by building the woman her own quarters in an out-of-the way place. Second Chronicles 8:11 says, "Solomon moved his wife, Pharaoh's daughter, from the City of David to the new palace he had built for her. He said, 'My wife must not live in King David's palace, for the Ark of the LORD has been there, and it is holy ground.'"

It was nice of Solomon to be concerned about holy ground. One only wishes he had been as concerned about God's holy Word.

But this is typical of sin managers. Instead of seeing sin as the problem, they see the awkwardness the sin creates as the problem and believe, therefore, that if they can find an answer for the awkwardness, they will have solved the problem.

Could there be any clearer sign of seduction?

Seriously, you know you're being seduced when one simple choice (repentance) would solve your problem completely, but you choose instead to embark on an arduous journey that's going to require you to be constantly juggling and maneuvering to avoid the fallout of whatever bad behavior you're trying to protect. In other words, when you choose sin management over repentance, you're choosing stress over peace, bondage over freedom, and danger over safety.

Think through four important aspects of this issue with me.

THE HEART OF THE SIN MANAGER

There's a lot of psychology in this world (some of it good and a lot of it bad) that attempts to explain people's behavior. But the Bible cuts through all the yammering and nails the central issue. Proverbs 4:23 says, "Guard your heart above all else, for it determines the course of your life."

Obviously, the "heart" in this verse is not the blood-pumping organ in your chest. It refers to the inner you, that place where your will, emotion, and intellect come together to form a little thing we call passion. Every man on earth is ultimately driven by his passion. Hence the warning: it determines the course of your life.

Think of the log flume ride at your favorite amusement park.

You settle down into the log thingy and away you go, gliding through the trough on a steady stream of moving water. Up, over, and around you float, with a dip here and a drop there, until you come to the grand finale: a dive and splashdown that is intended to leave you soaking wet.

You may never have thought about this before, but the course of your life is just as predictable as the path of an amusement park thrill ride. I hear people talk about not knowing what life will bring, and in terms of specific events that's true. But in terms of a general direction, it's not true. The message of Proverbs 4:23 is that whatever is in your heart creates a trough that you must follow. That's right, *must* follow. Whatever your will, emotion, and intellect agree on becomes your passion and the thing you will pursue. So when you see a guy choosing sin management over repentance, you know that sin (or the way it makes him feel) has become the dominant passion of his heart.

Solomon, for example, probably wasn't in love with his Egyptian wife. But he was in love with the idea of being a political mover and shaker. His driving passion was to be a major player on the world stage, and his treaty with the Egyptian pharaoh, which included the hand of the pharaoh's daughter in marriage, was a huge step toward that goal. It sent a message to the world that Solomon was ready to play ball with the big boys.

And you know what they say: you can't have too much of a good thing. So if one peace treaty accompanied by a foreign wife fed Solomon's passion, two would satisfy it even more. And if two, then three, and so on, until Solomon had hundreds of foreign wives roaming the royal hallways in their curlers and bunny slippers.

The problem arises when you begin to understand that passion for worldly things usurps any love you may think you have for God. Some guys claim that their sin has nothing to do with their love for God. A porn addict, for example, will often find solace in going to church and might even be a church leader. He tells himself that God is his first love and that his porn problem is, well, a problem for sure, but certainly doesn't negate his love for God. Or an adulterer may feel ashamed, but consoles himself with the notion that, in his heart of hearts, God is still number one in his life.

Not so fast.

Look at these words from the apostle John: "Do not love this world nor the things it offers you, for when you love the world, you do not have the love of the Father in you" (1 John 2:15).

In the category of cold, hard truths, this is a doozy: God doesn't share the throne of your heart with anybody or anything. You either give it to him wholly and completely, or he vacates it. You can tell yourself that God comes first and that the sin you're harboring is just a little something you need to work on, but if you choose a lifestyle of sin management over repentance, you've pledged your allegiance to your sin, not to God.

The throne of your heart is not a porch swing or a love seat. It doesn't offer enough space for two passions. This is what Jesus meant when he said that we can't serve two masters (Matt. 6:24), that God's promise to give us everything we need is contingent on us serving him "above all else" (Matt. 6:33), and that unless we repent we will perish (Luke 13:3). It's what Paul was talking about when he challenged us to separate ourselves from the things of this world (2 Cor. 6:17). And it's the heart of our Lord's message to the church at Laodicea: be either hot or cold, but whatever you do, don't be lukewarm (Rev. 3:15).

So this is where an understanding of the abomination we call sin management begins: with the knowledge that it always comes from a heart that is not right with God.

THE TOOLS OF THE SIN MANAGER

I'm not a tool guy, but the tool guys I know say that any job is easy if you have the right tools. This is a secondary but still very important reason why some guys opt for sin management over repentance. The tools at their disposal make sin management look like a safe option. Here are the five most common ones.

SIN MANAGEMENT TOOL #1: SEPARATION

Otherwise known as compartmentalization, separation is the act of building walls around your sin to keep it from contaminating other areas of your life. Solomon did this literally when he built a separate palace for his Egyptian wife.

This tactic reminds me of a guy I knew who wouldn't smoke in his house. He would sit on the back patio and smoke. He would walk around the yard and smoke. He would sit in his garage and smoke when it was raining. But he wouldn't smoke in his house because he didn't want to devalue his possessions by saturating them with the disgusting smell of stale smoke. He would eventually die a slow, agonizing death from lung cancer, but he could at least take solace in the fact that his drapes and furniture didn't stink.

The very idea of cordoning off areas of our lives to keep sin separated and contained is utter nonsense. The notion that it's okay for a man to get wasted as long as he does it on the weekend so it doesn't affect his work . . . or that it's okay for him to curse and tell dirty jokes as long as he doesn't do it in front of his kids . . . or that it's okay for him to watch porn as long as he does it when no one else is around is a fool's gambit for one major reason:

even if you could always keep the sin contained, you can't keep the effects of the sin contained.

The smoker I just mentioned, for example, may have smoked only outside his house, but he carried the effects of that smoking with him even when he was inside the house, and it eventually killed him. Or what about the guy who only watches porn when he's alone? Does it have any less of an effect on his thought life, the way he views women, or the way he interacts with his wife?

Of course not, because sin is so much more than just the act itself. It's the effect of the act on our hearts and minds and loved ones. King David, for example, committed adultery with Bathsheba in the privacy of his bedroom. Her husband was out of town. They were alone. Everything was nicely compartmentalized. But the effects of that sin reverberated like nothing David could have imagined and eventually brought him to some of the most painful and humiliating moments of his life.

It was the same with Solomon. Building a separate palace for his pagan wife may have cleaned up a public relations problem, but it further eroded his faithfulness to the Lord and led him to even more bad choices.

Bottom line: separation may put a more politically correct appearance on things, but it does nothing to help your broken relationship with God.

SIN MANAGEMENT TOOL #2: IMPERSONATION

Sin managers all understand the importance of impersonating a person who is *not* a sin manager. We know Solomon did this.

Read again the verse that exposes him as a sin manager: "Solomon moved his wife, Pharaoh's daughter, from the City of David to the new palace he had built for her. He said, 'My wife must not live in King David's palace, for the Ark of the LORD has been there, and it is holy ground'" (2 Chron. 8:11).

Now read the very next verse: "Then Solomon presented burnt offerings to the LORD on the altar he had built for him in front of the entry room of the Temple" (v. 12).

Don't miss the references to building in both verses. Apparently, at the same time Solomon was building a palace for his pagan wife, he was also building an altar to the living God. This is classic sin-manager technique. Like a magician who distracts you with one hand while he does the trick with the other, a sin manager involves himself in religious activity to draw your attention away from his sin.

King David used this tool. After sleeping with Bathsheba and impregnating her, he launched a heartless conspiracy to have her husband killed. One of the ways he covered his tracks was by continuing on with his sacrifices and prayers as if nothing were wrong.

This is why I'm never surprised when someone in the church gets caught in a scandal, even someone prominent like an elder or staff member. If you've made a commitment to sin management, it's imperative that you keep up the illusion of faithfulness to God. It's critical that you keep going to church and serving like someone who's not harboring a dirty little secret. Sometimes sin managers seem even more impassioned about their religion than they were before, not because they actually are, but because they feel the need to deflect attention away from what's really going on in their lives.

A number of years ago an individual in our church volunteered to lead our biggest service project of the year. It's a massive endeavor that involves almost half our congregation and requires intensive effort for about four months. We were delighted to have a volunteer, and especially to have one who was so well respected and who we knew could do the job. On the very day that the service project was scheduled to happen, we learned that this person was engaged in an extramarital affair. Naturally, the person was removed from the leadership role immediately, necessitating a mad scramble to pick up the slack so the event could go on. Later, people expressed amazement that the person would volunteer to lead the project while harboring such sin. But it really wasn't an odd thing at all. It's exactly the kind of thing sin managers do to cover their tracks.

SIN MANAGEMENT TOOL #3: MISREPRESENTATION

Hardly a month goes by that we don't see this tool being used on the national stage. You know the drill. A famous man is accused of doing something naughty or underhanded and immediately denies that it is what it looks like.

"That woman I was seen with that wasn't my wife? Oh, we're just friends."

"That drug test I failed? It was because of some cough medicine I took."

"That sexy text message I sent to my secretary? It was just a bad joke."

"That strip club I was at? I just stopped by to give my friend a ride home."

If confronted, the sin manager will use misrepresentation to convince the world that if it looks like a duck and walks like a duck and quacks like a duck, it is definitely not a duck.

In 1977, Jerry Sandusky, former assistant football coach at Penn State, established The Second Mile, a nonprofit charity for at-risk, underprivileged boys. Years later it would become known that Sandusky, a pedophile, used the charity to cultivate victims. In 2002, a Penn State graduate assistant in the football program happened to catch a glimpse of Sandusky in the shower with a young boy. The graduate assistant's impression was that something inappropriate was happening, so he reported what he saw to head football coach Joe Paterno. Almost a decade later we learned that what he saw was in fact a sexual assault in progress, but at the time Sandusky played it off as just a little boys-will-be-boys horsing around.

The maddening thing about this tool of misrepresentation is that it depends on the willful blindness of good people for its success. Yes, I said *willful blindness*. It is astonishing to me how perfectly intelligent people can look right at a duck and then later allow someone to convince them that what they saw wasn't a duck at all. The reason this happens is because people need for certain scenarios to be true in order to protect their well-ordered lives. A wife, for example, is so desperate to believe that her husband is not an adulterer that she will accept his lame excuses and flimsy denials. A university administration has millions of dollars and mountains of prestige to lose if one of its coaches is a pedophile, so it chooses to accept the "horseplay" explanation and monitor the situation instead of calling the police.

You've got to hand it to sin managers. They understand human nature. They know that if they can present their sin in terms that people want to believe, many of them will.

SIN MANAGEMENT TOOL #4: INTIMIDATION

Most sin managers eventually come to the place where even the most adept lie-telling and string-pulling isn't going to cut it. At that point they often forego trying to control appearances and public opinion and choose instead to try to control the people who know the truth.

Right now, all across America, employees from the assembly line to the boardroom are sitting on information that would expose corporate corruption. They are potential whistleblowers who, at any moment, could bring down high-profile companies, organizations, athletic programs, pastors, and politicians. And that's the problem. They are *potential* whistleblowers. The reason they're sitting on such explosive information is because they know the horrors they'll face if they speak up. They've been told they'll be fired, prosecuted, smeared, or, at the very least, subjected to the kind of intense media scrutiny that no one ever survives unscathed.

Sadly, intimidation doesn't happen in just the corporate world. Many abuse victims in the home, including helpless children, have been threatened with all manner of suffering if they tell anyone what's being done to them.

Of all the sin manager's tools, this one is by far the most reprehensible. It is emotional terrorism, pure and simple, and it takes the sin manager to a whole new level of depravity. It's one thing to commit a sin and try to cover it up. All of us have been there and done that to some degree. But to inflict additional terror on people—especially children—who have already suffered as a result of the sin itself is a special kind of evil.

SIN MANAGEMENT TOOL #5: MITIGATION

To mitigate a sin is to lighten or soften it, which is what the sin manager does when his first four tools don't work and he ends up getting busted. There are three ways to mitigate a sin.

One is to plead ignorance.

"I didn't know it was illegal."

"Nobody told me it was going to be *that* kind of party."

"I had no idea the prescription contained a banned substance."

The second way to mitigate a sin is to play the victim.

"I was just doing what I was told."

"She came on to me."

"She didn't tell me she was married."

And the third way to mitigate a sin is to trivialize it.

"I was just doing what everybody else does."

"Nobody got hurt."

"The whole thing is being blown out of proportion."

Mitigation, though used often, hardly ever works. Can you think of even one example of a person getting busted for something major, going into mitigation mode, and coming out on the other side looking brilliant? I can't. I can, however, think of many instances where a person's excuses made him seem silly and pathetic. Why, then, is mitigation so common? I'm not sure. Maybe the tendency to make excuses has been a part of our fallen nature from the beginning. (Remember what Adam said in the garden of Eden? "It was the woman who gave me the fruit!") Or perhaps sin management is addicting. Once you get started it's hard to stop, even when you reach the point of making a fool of yourself.

THE DOWNFALL OF THE SIN MANAGER

Some sin managers are, to be blunt, not very sharp and, therefore, doomed to fail from the get-go. Others are quite sharp and, one would think, very likely to succeed. However, history shows that the sharp sin managers are almost as likely to fail as the dull ones. Why? Because of a factor people seldom think about when they decide to become sin managers: sin management grows more difficult with each passing day. Consider the following facts.

DECEPTIONS BECOME MORE COMPLICATED AS TIME GOES ALONG

One day you tell a lie.

The next day you have to tell two more lies to make the original lie stand up before the scrutiny of a skeptic.

The next day you embellish the original lie in order to win sympathy from someone you'd like to have on your side.

The next day you tell another lie in answer to a question you didn't anticipate.

The next day someone asks you to clarify a detail in your original story, which requires yet another lie.

The next day . . .

You get the point. Sin management, because it relies so heavily on deception, grows increasingly complex as the days and weeks roll by. One lie leads to another, which leads to another, which leads to another. Before long, you've piled up so many lies you can't possibly remember them all. Many a sin manager is hung on the gallows of his own web of lies.

PEOPLE BECOME MORE SUSPICIOUS AS TIME GOES BY

In the early stages of a cover-up, the sin manager has a relatively easy time deceiving people because there's little or no reason for anyone to wonder if something illicit is going on. But as the awkward explanations, lame excuses, and "facts" that don't add up begin to, well, add up, people become increasingly suspicious.

Several years ago a woman came to see me who was worried her husband might be having an affair. As she explained the situation, she pulled a sheet of notebook paper out of her purse and handed it to me. The paper contained a long list of entries regarding unusual aspects of her husband's behavior:

Was 2 hours late getting home from work on 7/16.

Withdrew $100 from savings account on 7/19 without telling me.

Left for work an hour earlier than usual on 7/20. No explanation given.

Left work for 2 hours on the afternoon of 7/23. Did not answer cell phone during that period.

The list went on for a full page and covered a period of about two months. The woman explained that she started compiling the list only after her husband's routine became anything but. Suddenly the creature of habit she'd been living with for a decade and a half was keeping a schedule that had no consistency to it at all, except that it consistently produced pockets of time when he was unaccounted for and unreachable. She said she had no concrete proof that her husband was cheating and that he vehemently denied it. Still, because of the list I held in my hands, she was suspicious.

This is a typical scenario in the world of sin management. Noticeable changes in routine, mood, or job performance create suspicion, which exponentially increases the chances of the sin manager getting busted. Once the people you're trying to deceive start smelling a rat, your goose is as good as cooked. I've known wives who hired private investigators, retail managers who hired auditors, and business owners who installed surveillance cameras in their stores simply because of noticeable irregularities in a well-established routine.

MISTAKES BECOME MORE LIKELY AS TIME GOES ALONG

Obviously, if his web of lies is growing increasingly complex and his behavior is growing increasingly irregular, the sin manager's chance of making a mistake increases. But there's another reason why mistakes become more likely over time: sin managers often get lazy after a period of prolonged success.

Let's say, for example, that a man has an affair. If it's his first, you can bet he'll be extra cautious, like the kid who's only recently taken the training wheels off his bike. Every move will be carefully and thoughtfully executed. And then let's say four months later he pulls the plug on that affair without getting caught. From start to finish, he was able to hide it from his wife and everyone else who would want to wring his neck if they knew. I will guarantee you that the next time he decides to have an affair he will go into it with a cockier, more confident attitude than he had the first time. And if he gets away with it again and eventually there's a third time? He'll be like the kid riding his bicycle with no hands, eating a sandwich and waving to his friends.

Nothing breeds cockiness and complacency like success. And nothing breeds mistakes like cockiness and complacency.

GOD'S JUDGMENT GROWS MORE LIKELY AS TIME GOES ALONG

To my way of thinking, this fact is scarier than the first three put together. History shows again and again that God doesn't just sit back and watch sin managers operate like you and I might hunker down with some popcorn and watch a movie. He watches, yes, but he also reserves the right to get involved. And when he does, it's not pretty.

In Solomon's case, God started raising up enemies to oppose him (1 Kings 11:14, 23). In David's case, God sent the prophet Nathan to deliver a stinging rebuke and announce a series of dire punishments (2 Sam. 12:1–11). In Ananias and Sapphira's case, God just struck them dead (Acts 5:1–11).

This, then, is the ultimate miscalculation the sin manager makes. He thinks he's shrewd enough to keep the sin and the people in his life well managed. What he forgets to do is factor in a living God who sees everything, who doesn't take kindly to sin, and who, contrary to popular belief, isn't endlessly tolerant.

Right now, if you've been managing your sin, you need to understand that you are on thin ice. Don't tell me how well things are working out. I don't care if every move you've made has turned out beautifully so far. You're still on thin ice—and it's melting as we speak. The odds are overwhelming that you will eventually be exposed and shamed, either by a mistake, by some failure of your sin-management plan, or by a ruthless intervention of almighty God. You really only have one good option: repentance.

THE HOPE OF THE SIN MANAGER

Repentance is one of the most important and least understood commands in the Bible. Every time I talk with people who want to accept Christ, I ask them if they know what repentance is. They almost always say they do, but at least 70 percent of the time, they don't. They almost always define it as "being sorry for your sin." Certainly, there is an element of remorse involved, but true repentance is so much more than that.

Let's say I come home drunk one night and run over my neighbor's mailbox. The next morning I realize what I've done and feel terrible. So I go to my neighbor and apologize. Then I go buy him a new mailbox and install it. In fact, I buy him a better mailbox than he had before so that he now has the nicest mailbox in town.

Have I repented?

I've shown remorse and made restitution, yes. But have I repented?

Not if I go out and get drunk again the next night.

By definition, repentance is a change of mind that leads to a change in behavior. One of my favorite Scripture passages about repentance is 1 Corinthians 6:9–11: "Do you not know that the wicked will not inherit the kingdom of God? Do not be deceived: Neither the sexually immoral nor idolaters nor adulterers nor male prostitutes nor homosexual offenders nor thieves nor the greedy nor drunkards nor slanderers nor swindlers will inherit the kingdom of God. *And that is what some of you were*" (NIV, author's emphasis).

Repentance is not what saves us; grace is. But repentance is a response to grace that makes what we are after having received grace different from what we were before.

Here, then, is the tension between repentance and sin management. Repentance concerns itself with how things *are* while sin management only worries about how things *look*.

Think of a messy closet.

Repentance cleans out the closet.

Sin management straightens up the closet.

Repentance throws away the junk.

Sin management rearranges the junk.

Repentance gives you a better closet.

Sin management only gives you a better-looking closet.

What junk do you need to throw away?

One of my favorite repentance stories is about baseball Hall of Famer Dennis Eckersley. The guy could flat-out pitch. One of my favorite "Eck" stats is that he shut out the world champion Oakland A's in his first big league start and set a major league record by not allowing an earned run until his twenty-ninth inning.

But Dennis Eckersley, for a long period of his life, was a drunk. And not a lovable one. One time when his wife was out of town working, he and his daughter, Mandee, were staying at his wife's sister's house in Connecticut. During that visit, Dennis got drunk and became as boorish as he'd ever been. His sister-in-law, in what turned out to be a stroke of brilliance, started filming him without his knowledge.

The next morning when Dennis staggered down the stairs, he found the video playing on the television. Horrified, he asked his sister-in-law to turn it off. She refused. He begged and pleaded, but she let the tape roll on, allowing it to grind shame and embarrassment into his soul like a wingtip heel on a cigarette butt. Later, Dennis would refer to that experience as his wake-up call, the thing that motivated him to clean out his closet instead of just constantly rearranging its contents.[1]

If you're a sin manager, I plead with you to repent before you come to your own moment of humiliation. Don't be fooled by the success you've had keeping your life compartmentalized and your friends and family members in the dark. Sooner or later you'll make a mistake or God himself will get fed up and bring you down.

But don't take my word for it.

Consider the warning of the guy who wrote the book on sin management. None other than Solomon himself said, "People who conceal their sins will not prosper, but if they confess and turn from them, they will receive mercy" (Prov. 28:13).

WAKE-UP CALL № 6

YOU KNOW YOU'RE BEING SEDUCED WHEN YOUR FAITHFUL FRIENDS ARE TROUBLED BY YOUR BEHAVIOR

WHEN SOLOMON BECAME THE KING OF ISRAEL, HE INHERITED EVERY-thing his father, David, the former king, had left behind. This included both enemies and allies. Perhaps the best ally he inherited was King Hiram of Tyre: "King Hiram of Tyre had always been a loyal friend of David. When Hiram learned that David's son Solomon was the new king of Israel, he sent ambassadors to congratulate him" (1 Kings 5:1).

Solomon, ever the wise politician, wasn't about to let that alliance grow stale. In a move that would pay enormous dividends, he sent the following letter to Hiram:

"You know that my father, David, was not able to build a Temple to honor the name of the LORD his God because of the many wars waged against him by surrounding nations. He could not build until the LORD gave him victory over all his enemies. But now the LORD my God has given me peace on every side; I have no enemies, and all is well. So I am planning to build a Temple to honor the name of the LORD my God, just as he had instructed my father, David. For the LORD told him, 'Your son, whom I will place on your throne, will build the Temple to honor my name.'

"Therefore, please command that cedars from Lebanon be cut for me. Let my men work alongside yours, and I will pay your men whatever wages you ask. As you know, there is no one among us who can cut timber like you Sidonians!" (vv. 3–6)

As you can see from the last sentence, Solomon wasn't above using flattery to get what he wanted. Not that he needed to. Offering to pay someone whatever wages he asks for pretty much guarantees that you'll be doing business together. And so, upon receiving the message, a practically giddy Hiram said, "Praise the LORD today for giving David a wise son to be king of the great nation of Israel" (v. 7).

Eventually the schmoozing stopped and the two men got down to business. They signed a formal peace treaty and put their people to work. Before long, cedar and cypress timber was rolling into Israel, and wheat and olive oil were rolling into Tyre. Later, Hiram would also become Solomon's source for gold.

It's important to note that this happy arrangement was in effect for the entire twenty years it took Solomon to complete both his palace and the temple. Twenty years is a long time to be friends. You'd think that if two people were good friends for twenty years they'd be way past having to worry about the petty grievances that put so many friendships on the rocks. But when you're being seduced, as Solomon was, you start to think and act differently. Hence, this odd entry into the narrative:

It took Solomon twenty years to build the LORD's Temple and his own royal palace. At the end of that time, he gave twenty towns in the land of Galilee to King Hiram of Tyre. (Hiram had previously provided all the cedar and cypress timber and gold that Solomon had requested.) But when Hiram came from Tyre to see the towns Solomon had given him, he was not at all pleased with them. "What kind of towns are these, my brother?" he asked. So Hiram called that area Cabul (which means "worthless"), as it is still known today. (1 Kings 9:10–13)

For some reason, Solomon felt compelled to alter the arrangement he had with Hiram. Before, he had paid for the timber and gold with food. Now, suddenly, he's paying with real estate, which seems to have been fine with Hiram, until he saw the twenty towns Solomon gave him.

Imagine going on a blind date. Your best friend is fixing you up, so you have complete confidence that he's lined up a really attractive girl. You're so anxious to meet her you can barely contain yourself. But when you get to her house, out steps the homeliest girl you've ever seen. That's exactly how Hiram felt when he saw the real estate Solomon was giving him. The towns were so undesirable that Hiram dubbed the entire area "worthless," which apparently wasn't an exaggeration because the name stuck.

But it's Hiram's question to Solomon that I want you to notice. He said, "What kind of towns are these, my brother?" The two words that best describe the emotion behind that question are *disappointment* and *confusion*. Hiram can't believe his eyes. Further, he can't believe that his oldest and most trusted friend, a man who was like a brother to him, would so blatantly rip him off after decades of mutually beneficial commerce.

Why did Solomon do it?

There's the obvious fact that he didn't need Hiram's timber and gold as he once did, and therefore didn't feel as obligated to keep paying top dollar for it. But the deeper reality is that Solomon just wasn't the same guy he'd been twenty years earlier when he first struck the deal with Hiram. At this point the seduction of his heart had been in process for several years, making him gradually more selfish and materialistic. He was still a long way from rock bottom, but this transaction is a clear indication that he had changed, and not for the better.

HOW GOOD FRIENDS GO BAD

Good friends go bad noisily. They give off signals right and left, saying and doing things that leave the person on the other end of the relationship to try to make sense of it all. Hiram's question to Solomon—"What kind of towns are these, my brother?"—is much deeper than it seems. Hiram isn't really asking about the towns. He can see for himself what kind of towns they are. He's asking about Solomon. "What's up with you, my brother?" is closer to what he really means.

If ever a friend looks you in the eye and says, "What's up with you?" don't blow him off. Take the question seriously, because your friend wouldn't be asking if he couldn't see something alarming in your behavior. Allow me to list the top ten behaviors that will trigger suspicion in your friends.

SUSPICION TRIGGER #1: YOU STOP DOING SOMETHING YOU'VE ALWAYS DONE

All healthy relationships are built on consistent patterns of thought and behavior. You don't have to think or act alike in order to become friends with someone (remember, opposites attract!), but you do need to be able to count on consistency in the other person. A woman, for example, is unlikely to fall in love with a man who is affectionate one day and mean the next. One of the reasons Hiram and Solomon had such a good relationship is that for twenty years they stuck to a mutually agreeable pattern of behavior. Hiram provided lumber and gold in return for Solomon's wheat and olive oil. The day Solomon deviated from that pattern was the day Hiram became confused and began to wonder what was going on.

As a pastor, I understand this all too well. I've had good friends who were solid church members suddenly drop out of the fellowship with no warning and no explanation. I've had productive coworkers who suddenly became disinterested and ineffective. I've counseled parents who were wild with worry because their straight-A student was suddenly bringing home Ds and Fs. In each and every case, the suspicion was justified. The unusual behavior indicated that trouble was afoot.

Whether we want to admit it or not, most of us are creatures of habit. We settle into patterns of thought and behavior that fit our temperaments and worldviews, that the people around us get used to, and that our friends learn to like. Naturally, when we stop doing what we've always done, those friends get suspicious.

SUSPICION TRIGGER #2: YOU START DOING SOMETHING YOU'VE NEVER DONE

Can you say "midlife crisis"?

This is the guy who breaks out of his well-established patterns of thought and behavior and ventures in the other direction. Instead of only quitting this or that, he starts adding things to his life that seem completely out of character: a hot new car, a hip new wardrobe, a ponytail, a tattoo, an earring, or a mistress.

Experts say that guys who go down this road are trying to hang on to their fading youth, trying to prove to themselves that they've still got it, or trying to capture feelings and experiences they missed out on when they were younger before it's too late. The problem is that the guy is no longer a teenager trying to stretch his wings and find his place in the world. He's a grown man with a job and a family that depends on him. And so, instead of fooling around in the backseat on a date because he's curious about sex, he's having a full-blown affair and jeopardizing his marriage, his relationship with his kids, his reputation, and possibly even his career.

One time a middle-aged guy in our church stopped cutting his hair and started wearing an earring. The general consensus was that he looked silly in a ponytail, though no one wanted to tell him to his face. One day I happened to be chatting with him and said, "What's with the new look?" He said, "Nothing, really. I just always wanted long hair and decided I better grow it out before it's all gone."

Fair enough.

But I also asked his wife in private what she thought about his new look. She shook her head and rolled her eyes. I said, "Is there anything besides long hair and an earring that has crept into his life?" She said, "Not as far as I can tell. But you can bet I'm keeping my eyes open."

Smart woman.

SUSPICION TRIGGER #3: YOU GIVE LAME ANSWERS TO SERIOUS QUESTIONS

"How did that lipstick get on your shirt?"

"What lipstick?"

"*That* lipstick."

"Oh. Um, that isn't lipstick."

"Then what is it?"

"I was, uh, giving a presentation at work and I, uh, was using a red marker on the white board."

"It doesn't look like a red marker; it looks like lipstick."

"Oh, it's definitely a red marker."

"Okay then, why does your shirt smell like a woman's perfume?"

"It doesn't."

"It does too. And it's not the kind I use."

"I, uh . . . oh yes, a couple of the women on our team gave me a hug after the presentation."

"Because it was so wonderful?"

"I guess so."

This conversation really happened. A wife shared it with me a few years ago when she came to tell me that she thought her husband was having an affair. Interestingly, her anger wasn't directed at the affair as much as it was at her husband's refusal to tell her the truth. The lame response he gave about the lipstick was one of several he'd given her. She said, "If he thinks I'm unattractive, fine. But it really hurts that he thinks I'm also stupid."

People who are being seduced have to give lame answers to serious questions because, short of the truth, there aren't any good answers to explain their foolish behavior. Solomon, who likely gave more than a few lame answers during his descent into seduction, was probably speaking from experience when he said, "The mouths of fools are their ruin; they trap themselves with their lips" (Prov. 18:7).

SUSPICION TRIGGER #4: YOU'RE MORE VOLATILE THAN USUAL

Stress is a fact of life, especially if you're a male between the ages of thirty-five and fifty-five. Those are your peak weight-carrying years. You likely carry the weight of a job, a family, and a host of cultural expectations.

Speaking of cultural expectations, how's your testosterone level? I'm sure you've thought about it. You can't watch TV (especially a sporting event) without seeing a commercial that asks point blank if your energy level and libido are up to par. It's just one of a thousand ways our culture puts pressure on men. Then when you throw the kind of seduction that is the subject of this book on top of all that cultural pressure, you really have a powder keg.

And *powder keg* is the right term because one of the main indicators of stress overload is the angry outburst. Pressure builds and builds and builds and eventually has to blow. As you might expect, this is often when a wife realizes something serious is going on inside her husband. A hole punched in the drywall or a flurry of curse words from a normally even-tempered guy is hard for even the most optimistic woman to ignore.

SUSPICION TRIGGER #5: YOU'RE LESS PASSIONATE THAN USUAL

One thing you can say about guys is that we care about things. Not always the right things, but we do have a lot of passion to give to the things that interest us. Why do you think sports teams slap their logos on everything from T-shirts to key chains? In my own closet I have, at this moment, twenty shirts that have a St. Louis Cardinals, Mizzou Tigers, Tampa Bay Buccaneers, or Orlando Magic logo on them. (That doesn't include all the ball caps, coffee mugs, lounge pants, socks, DVDs, magazines, etc.) I say "at this moment" because by the time this book is published there will be more. I know, I know . . . I do not need this many shirts from my favorite teams. My wife has pointed this out to me, and she's right. Her point is, however, beside the point. I am a guy and I *have* to buy gear from my favorite teams.

This is why advertisers of everything from razor blades to automobiles use scantily clad models. It's why there are so many sports bars and action movies and video games. It's why stores like Bass Pro Shop and Dick's Sporting Goods are the size of small countries. It's why there are millions of porn sites on the

Internet. Everybody knows guys are loaded with passion and will spare no effort or expense in chasing down the objects of that passion, which is why a sudden drop in passion is so noticeable and alarming.

A good, goal-oriented student suddenly wants to drop out of school.

A career-minded businessman suddenly wants to quit his job.

A devout churchgoer suddenly prefers to sleep in on Sunday mornings.

A bedroom Casanova suddenly loses interest in sex.

Who wouldn't wonder what was going on with these guys?

SUSPICION TRIGGER #6: YOU MANAGE YOUR TIME DIFFERENTLY

Time management is one of the main keys to success in life. The people who manage it well tend to prosper, and those who don't tend to fail. The point, however, is not just that good time managers get more done. The point is that your management of time offers a peek into your soul. It reveals your priorities. You can make any claim you want about what's important to you, but the things you give your time to will be your real priorities. That's why a change in the way you manage your time is so significant. It reveals a shift in your thinking, a shift in what you believe is important. It screams, "Something has changed!"

Obviously, a shift toward better priorities will raise no red flags. You'll likely be hailed as a hero by your loved ones. But giving more time to your job and less to your family will raise alarms, especially if the longer working hours seem contrived. For example, if you haven't had to work late more than two or three times in the last year, but suddenly you're working late two or three nights a week, you can expect some questions from your wife.

I read once that the time management issue is usually the first indicator a wife gets that her husband is cheating. From there she may notice everything from calls on his cell phone to lipstick on his collar, but it often starts with changes in how or where he spends his time. Or whom he spends it with.

SUSPICION TRIGGER #7: YOU MANAGE YOUR MONEY DIFFERENTLY

"Follow the money."

Since the phrase was used in the 1976 motion picture *All the President's Men*, people have been using it any time there's a whiff of scandal in the air.

Does something seem fishy?

Follow the money.

Are people behaving strangely?

Follow the money.

Are facts not adding up?

Follow the money.

It's good advice because money is involved in just about everything we do, especially the things we do wrong. One website lists the top ten things you should never put on your credit card. Among them are alcoholic beverages, adult toys, pornography, hotel rooms used for cheating, lottery tickets, cash advances, and binge shopping. The website also offers suggestions on how to hide your naughty purchases from the people in your life who might object.

Jesus said, "Wherever your treasure is, there the desires of your heart will also be" (Matt. 6:21). The statement is equally true if you reverse it: whatever the desires of your heart are, there your treasure will also be.

SUSPICION TRIGGER #8: YOU DISTANCE YOURSELF FROM FAMILY AND FRIENDS

Close relationships are a wonderful thing . . . until you start down the path of sin. Then, suddenly, those people become the biggest threats to the so-called happiness that you've begun to chase.

Because they love you, they start trying to reel you back in. They beg. They plead. They try to talk sense into you. Failing that, they use guilt. Better to make you feel like a bum and save your soul than to watch you throw your life away.

Why do you think the prodigal son moved to a far country (Luke 15:13)? Did he have to in order to find the wild life he longed to experience? Of course not. He moved to a far country to get away from family and friends who would have given him a hard time about his choices.

But distance doesn't have to involve miles. You can distance yourself from someone even while living in the same house or working in the same building. How? By smiling less. By talking less. By criticizing more. It happens all the time. Many of the people I've counseled over the years have come to me initially because someone close to them—usually a spouse or a child—started building walls. Invisible walls, yes, but still as effective as if they were made out of bricks and mortar.

SUSPICION TRIGGER #9: YOU FLIP EVERY DIFFICULT CONVERSATION

"Honey, I've noticed you've been a little irritable lately."

"*Me*? What about *you*? I came home from work this afternoon and the first thing you did was jump on me about not getting the lawn mowed over the weekend."

"I didn't jump on you. I just mentioned that it needed to be mowed before it rains."

"See, that's what you always do. You jump on me about something and then say you didn't, like I just dreamed it or something."

"All I'm trying to say is that it seems like something is stressing you out. This conversation is a good example of what I'm talking about."

"I'll tell you what's stressing me out. You nitpicking me all the time. That's what really gets on my nerves."

People who know they are drifting off course become very defensive. They see every question as an attack that needs to be repelled. And since they can't defend themselves with honest answers, they opt for a counteroffensive. They figure that if they're loud and aggressive enough, their attackers will retreat. They're usually right.

The problem, of course, is the big picture. You've heard the old saying about winning the battle but losing the war? That's what happens to people who employ this strategy. They succeed in the moment while at the same time adding credence to the accusation being made against them.

SUSPICION TRIGGER #10: YOU BECOME NICER THAN YOU'VE EVER BEEN

In our area it's not unusual to see somebody selling roses out of the trunk of his beat-up car. He's usually parked on the shoulder under an overpass. He has a sign taped to the side of his rattletrap that says "Roses $5 a Dozen!" And yes, he's usually working a deal with some guy who has pulled over on his way home from work. That's right—some guy. It's always a guy. As far as I know, there's no law that says women can't buy flowers, but I have never seen a woman buying flowers from a roadside vendor.

I always assume the customer is either a) in trouble with his wife and hoping to smooth things over with some roses, or b) cheating on her and trying not to seem like a cheater. I realize the latter is rather pessimistic, but I've counseled enough couples to know that it's a very realistic possibility. I can't count the times I've heard a wife say, "I knew he was up to something when he brought me flowers for no reason." Or "when he offered to give me a back rub." Or "when he brought me breakfast in bed." Anytime an insensitive clod suddenly becomes Mr. Considerate, his wife is going to wonder what's going on.

Years ago I counseled a couple that was trying to put their marriage back together after the husband's affair. The wife, who had quite a sense of humor, turned to her husband and said, "I liked you better when you were cheating on me. You were a lot nicer then."

THE BIG QUESTION

So now comes the big question: Are any of the ten scenarios I just described a reality in your life? Do you have your own personal Hirams looking at your odd behavior and saying, "What's up with you?" If so, there are a couple of hard truths you need to think about.

HARD TRUTH #1: TRUE FRIENDS' SUSPICIONS ARE ALMOST ALWAYS JUSTIFIED

The typical response when we sense suspicion being directed our way is to blow it off. We laugh, as if the mere idea is the funniest thing we've ever heard. We tell our loved ones they're imagining things, they've seen too many movies, or they've misinterpreted the facts. And yet, our friends are not stupid. They know that normal people don't suddenly become weird for no reason. Respectful people don't suddenly become rebellious for no reason. Trustworthy people don't suddenly become undependable for no reason. Happy people don't suddenly become moody for no reason.

Now you might say, "But Mark, what if I really do believe the suspicion being directed toward me is unjustified?" In that case, there are two possibilities. The less likely of the two is that you're right and, for whatever reason, your loved ones really are imagining things. The more likely possibility is that you have a blind spot. A blind spot is some flaw in yourself that everyone in the world can see but you.

A number of years ago, as part of an evangelistic campaign, another preacher and I paid a visit to a woman who had been in the Miss America pageant a few years earlier. I was looking forward to the visit, figuring the woman would be beautiful and articulate. She was, but I didn't enjoy the visit because from the moment we stepped into her home, we were harassed by her dog, which was some sort of pit bull mix.

I had taken a seat on the couch and crossed one leg over the other when the dog came tearing into the room, barking and growling like a demon straight out of hell. You might know that, of the two strangers in the house, the dog decided to eat me first. When I saw it galloping my way, I left my leg crossed as a kind of buffer and braced myself. The dog skidded to a stop and stuck his head up through the opening in my crossed legs so that his chin was resting on my crotch. His teeth were bared. Saliva was dripping from his jowls and he was growling.

At that moment I understood the meaning of abject terror.

I saw children and grandchildren that I would never have passing before my eyes.

My only hope was that our hostess, the lovely and beautiful young woman who looked like a movie star, would call off her dog or, better yet, wrestle him away from me. She didn't. Instead, she laughed. Hysterically. And then she said, "Aw, he likes you!"

I was so frightened I couldn't speak.

Finally sensing my fear, she said, "Just stick your hand down and let him lick it. Once he tastes you, he'll be fine."

I kid you not, that's what she said.

So, I did. I figured it was either that or . . . well, you know.

Do I need to state the obvious here?

That woman, as gorgeous as she was, had a blind spot: her dog. Some people are more self-aware than others, but probably everybody has at least one blind spot at any given moment. It's probably also safe to say that blind spots come and go as we write the various chapters of our lives. Several times in my life Marilyn has pointed out something in me that I didn't see in myself. My first reaction when she does that is always to argue, but in every case I end up admitting she's right. And here's the funny thing. Once it's pointed out and explained to me, I can see it plain as day.

I'll leave it to the psychologists to explain how perfectly intelligent people can be blind to their own foibles. For now, just understand that it happens all the time, and it may explain why you're mystified by the suspicion that's being directed toward you.

Understand this, however: your suspicious friends are probably not wrong, any more than Hiram was about Solomon. You know, I know, we all know that where there's smoke, there's fire. Instead of denying it, you'd best get busy fixing it.

HARD TRUTH #2: YOU COULD BE DOING IRREPARABLE HARM

First Corinthians 13:7 says, "Love . . . endures through every circumstance." How true. I've seen women put up with years of abuse. I've seen parents continue to help adult children who brought them nothing but heartache. I've seen friends set aside betrayals that would have caused major feuds between casual acquaintances.

But while love endures through every circumstance, that doesn't mean it will put up with mistreatment forever. Sometimes, even though you love somebody, you have to walk away. You have to separate yourself from the source of the pain. Solomon said it in Proverbs 18:19: "Arguments separate friends like a gate locked with bars." Notice he didn't say that arguments necessarily *end* a friendship, only that they separate friends. The problem becomes such an obstacle to healthy interaction that distance becomes the only answer.

In my experience, there's no human being more pitiful than the man who has destroyed his most precious possession, only to realize it after the damage was done. I've seen guys big enough to play defensive tackle in the NFL bury their faces in their hands and cry like babies because their wives and children had left them. And I always wonder: *Why didn't you think about this when you were acting like a jerk and your wife was begging you to change?*

Recently, I spoke with a man whose wife had just left him. They'd had a rocky relationship for a long time, so no one was really surprised—except the man himself. He said, "I can't believe she left." I said, "But you guys have been having trouble for the last couple of years. She's been begging you to go to counseling and you refused. Why are you so surprised?" He gave me a bewildered look and said, "I just didn't think things were that bad."

Another guy I know got fired from his job. He felt that he'd been mistreated and was railing against his boss. I was sympathizing with him until he mentioned in passing that he'd been given a warning. I said, "Wait. You were given a warning?" He said, "Yeah, they wrote me up a couple of times because of a problem I was having with another employee."

Guys, what is it with us that we can't see the handwriting on the wall?

Let me just say it as plainly as I know how.

If your behavior is causing the people who love you to wonder what's up with you, you're already in trouble. You can bet that a wife or a friend or an employer who is suspicious of you is already envisioning worst-case scenarios and mulling contingency plans. You may be sitting there thinking you're a long way from real trouble. Don't be too sure. With every day that passes—with every inconsiderate act—you could be creating a little more distance in the relationship. One day you might wake up and discover that the distance has become insurmountable.

In ancient Israel, suspicion was taken very seriously. In Numbers 5:29–30, the Lord says to Moses: "This, then, is the law of jealousy when a woman goes astray and defiles herself while married to her husband, or when feelings of jealousy come over a man because he suspects his wife. The priest is to have her stand before the LORD and is to apply this entire law to her" (NIV).

What is the "entire law" the Lord refers to? It's spelled out in the prior verses, 11–28. It involved taking the suspected party before the priest with an offering and then presenting her to "stand trial before the LORD." The woman had to take an oath and drink bitter water that would bring a curse upon her if her husband's suspicions were justified.

It's easy to read a passage like this and get distracted by the details. Suddenly we're arguing about gender equality and curses instead of seeing what God was really trying to do. This law and many others were clearly designed to keep the Israelite nation morally pure.

I find it interesting that God, in addition to all his specific commands, gave special consideration to the problem of suspicion, that sick feeling you get in your gut when someone you love starts acting weird.

Suspicion is a serious matter to God.

It ought to be to us too.

WAKE-UP CALL №7

YOU KNOW YOU'RE BEING SEDUCED WHEN YOUR DRINKING GLASSES COST MORE THAN SOME PEOPLE'S HOUSES

LIFE HAS A KNACK FOR PRODUCING INTERESTING COINCIDENCES. Like right now, for instance.

As I sit down to start writing this chapter on materialism, it's Black Friday, unquestionably the most materialistic day of the year in America. I didn't plan it this way. Honest, I didn't. It just came to pass in the normal flow of my writing schedule. I'll admit it did occur to me that, in light of this unusual confluence of circumstances, I ought to drag my laptop to the mall and write in the middle of all that unbridled greed. Surely there would be some inspiration to be found among all those obsessive shoppers dragging their treasures up and down the concourse. In the end, though, I opted for my home office. It was easier to find a parking space.

If anyone in the ancient world would have dug Black Friday, it's Solomon. In fact, it's no stretch to say that, for him, every day was Black Friday. By his own admission, he lived his life on a relentless quest to acquire as much stuff as possible. He wrote:

I also tried to find meaning by building huge homes for myself and by planting beautiful vineyards. I made gardens and parks, filling them with all kinds of fruit trees. I built reservoirs to collect the water to irrigate my many flourishing groves. I bought slaves, both men and women, and others were born into my household. I also owned large herds and flocks, more than any of the kings who had lived in Jerusalem before me. I collected great sums of silver and gold, the treasure of many kings and provinces. I hired wonderful singers, both men and women, and had many beautiful concubines. I had everything a man could desire! (Eccl. 2:4–8)

You might say, "But what's the big deal? Aren't kings supposed to be rich?"

Of course, but even a casual reading of Solomon's story reveals an unhealthy obsession with material things. He wasn't content to be rich in the way kings are normally rich. He wanted to break new ground, to reach a level of wealth no king had ever experienced before.

Again, you might say, "But didn't God promise him riches?"

He sure did, in 1 Kings 3:13. But I've yet to find one scholar who believes Solomon's all-out obsession with material things pleased God. In fact, the big problem with Solomon's wealth was that it was so obviously *not* godly, either in its acquisition or its application. As I've already pointed out, Solomon gained much of his wealth by burdening the people with heavy taxation and harsh labor demands (1 Kings 12:4). He also flaunted his wealth, like the time he offered to the Lord a sacrifice of 22,000 cattle and 120,000 sheep and goats (1 Kings 8:63). Talk about overkill! Especially when it's not even the blood of animals that God really desires, a fact Solomon's own father, David, knew very well (Ps. 51:16–17).

But the verse that stands out in my mind as the clearest

indicator of Solomon's obsession with all things lavish is 1 Kings 10:21: "All of King Solomon's drinking cups were solid gold, as were all the utensils in the Palace of the Forest of Lebanon. They were not made of silver, for silver was considered worthless in Solomon's day!"

Solid gold drinking cups?

Wow.

As I write these words, gold is selling for $1,751.55 an ounce. Let's be conservative and say that a drinking cup like Solomon used weighed twelve ounces. That would make his drinking cups worth $21,018.60 apiece in today's dollars. A set of six would cost well over a hundred grand.

I'll say it again. Wow.

And keep in mind, Solomon's drinking cups were a mere drop in the bucket of his overall wealth. Second Chronicles 9:13–28 details his obsession with gold, starting with the fact that he received about twenty-five tons of gold per year, not counting the additional revenue he received from merchants and traders. He ordered his craftsmen to make virtually everything out of gold. Even his throne, which was made out of ivory, was overlaid with pure gold, making it like no other throne in the world (2 Chron. 9:19).

But gold wasn't Solomon's only obsession.

He also appears to have had a thing for horses. A *big* thing, judging from the fact that he owned twelve thousand of them. Even granting that a horse was the ancient equivalent of the modern-day automobile and that it wouldn't be unusual for a king to own several, still, twelve thousand?

And then there was his harem, of course, which everybody's heard about and which I'll address at length in the next chapter.

The main reason why we know all this wealth was not of God (even though he promised to give Solomon riches), is the fact it stands in direct violation of God's command in Deuteronomy 17:16–17: "The king must not build up a large stable of horses for himself or send his people to Egypt to buy horses, for the LORD has told you, 'You must never return to Egypt.' The king must not take many wives for himself, because they will turn his heart away from the LORD. And he must not accumulate large amounts of wealth in silver and gold for himself."

Solomon's descent into turbocharged materialism is one of the most striking aspects of his seduction. Sadly, a lot of guys today follow the same path. No, they don't accumulate anywhere near the kind of wealth that Solomon accumulated, but that's not the point. Materialism isn't about your balance sheet; it's about your heart. You can be dirt poor and still be materialistic if your heart is set on material things. I'm simply saying that a lot of men get caught up in the pursuit of wealth to the point that it begins to cloud their judgment. They start making choices that are more career-oriented and less family-oriented. They start making risky investments. They start bending rules or downright cheating to get ahead. And, worst of all, they start viewing themselves through the lens of materialism, comparing themselves to their peers and judging their success purely on the basis of material accomplishments.

WHY PEOPLE BECOME MATERIALISTIC

Clearly, not everyone is materialistic. Mother Teresa, for example, was offered multiple opportunities to become a kind of international ambassador of goodwill. As such, she would have lived the life of a celebrity. She would have traveled the world, stayed in the finest hotels, eaten the finest food, written books, given speeches, and met with heads of state. She simply wasn't interested. Her work in the filthy back alleys of Calcutta was more important to her.

So it's a fair question. Why do some people become materialistic? Let me suggest four reasons.

REASON #1: AFFINITY

Let's face it. We're materialistic from the moment we draw our first breath. We're obsessed with comfort, which, at that point, means a full tummy, some cuddling, and a clean diaper. It may not sound like much, but for seven measly pounds of helpless tissue, it's a start. From there we become obsessed with our mommies, our bottles, our toys, our sibling's toys, and just about anything colorful and shiny. We're reaching for and grabbing everything we can get our hands on and crying for those things that are out of reach. Who can deny that we're born with a strong affinity for materialism?

Ideally, our moms and dads begin right away to suppress that materialistic bent. The word *no* is most helpful in this endeavor. In the old days a well-timed swat on the rump or slap on the wrist was considered acceptable, though now such methods are frowned upon by the politically correct crowd. (You know who they are. They're the ones in the restaurant trying to have a reasonable discussion with their kicking and screaming four-year-olds.)

And then of course there are those parents who, by their example, pretty much give their kids lessons in how to be materialistic. As I pointed out at the beginning of this chapter, I'm writing this on Black Friday. Watch any newscast on this day and you'll see a live report from the toy department of some discount store. You'll hear the reporter talk about this year's hottest toys and how the stores have hired off-duty police officers to keep fights from breaking out as parents desperately scramble to make sure their kids don't have to return to school in the new year without Christmas gift bragging rights. On Christmas morning those parents will proudly tell their stories about what they had to go through to ensure such a wonderful Christmas for their children, as if Christmas wouldn't have been wonderful at all without those toys.

Can you say "double whammy"?

We're born with an affinity for materialism, and then some of us have materialistic parents who pour fuel on the fire. These two facts alone are enough to make most of the population materialistic.

REASON #2: AIMLESSNESS

Do you remember the reason Solomon gave for his nosedive into the deep end of materialism? He said he was trying to find meaning (Eccl. 2:4).

I've known quite a few people who were struggling with the meaning of life. (We preachers meet them like bartenders meet alcoholics.) And they all have something in common: they can't settle on a purpose or a direction to devote themselves to. They can't name anything they're passionate about. Even Solomon in Ecclesiastes described his life as being "meaningless" and like "chasing the wind" (1:14). A lot of the people who feel this way are going to binge on something in an effort to create some excitement. It'll often be pleasure or stuff. Or pleasure *and* stuff.

Jesus told a story about a young man who demanded his share of his father's estate and went off to live in a far country where he squandered it all on what he called "wild living" (Luke 15:13). The Bible doesn't say the young man felt his life had become meaningless, but what else are we to conclude? Apparently, working for his father had become tedious. He must have thought, *I don't think I can do this for the rest of my life. There's got to be something better out there.*

By the way, there's nothing inherently wrong with this feeling. Some people arrive at such a place and use it as a springboard to greater accomplishment. But many go the other way. They do what Solomon did. They try to find fulfillment by cramming the empty spaces in their lives full of stuff.

REASON #3: ACCESSIBILITY

Solomon makes another telling comment in Ecclesiastes 2:10: "Anything I wanted, I would take." Isn't it harder to restrain yourself when everything you want is within reach?

I'm old enough to remember the days when, if you wanted to look at porn, you had to visit a newsstand or be close enough to a large city to sneak into an X-rated theater. Millions of people living in small towns had neither option. But then along came VCRs. All of a sudden you could rent naughty movies and bring them home. Even our small-town video store at the time had a mysterious back room you could enter if you were twenty-one or older. And then along came the Internet, which eliminated the need for the video store and the risk of being seen slipping into that back room. Now you can even watch porn on your phone if you feel so inclined. Is it any wonder so many more people are addicted to porn these days?

When something enticing is within reach, it's hard not to grab it. And really, what isn't within reach anymore? With credit cards and delayed billing and no interest for five years, just about anybody can have anything they want.

When Marilyn and I first got married, virtually everything we owned was a hand-me-down from our parents. When we get out our old picture albums, I see the furniture in our first campus apartment and remember it from my parents' house when I was about twelve years old. We had secondhand stuff because we couldn't afford anything else. Nowadays, young people get married and move into new homes loaded with new furniture. But not because they're wealthy! They just happen to live in a generation when just about anybody can get credit.

REASON #4: AFFIRMATION

Every time you have a materialistic impulse, someone or something will be there to affirm it . . . to assure you that, no, you're not a bad person for having the "itch" and that, yes, it's okay to scratch it.

Take your typical shopaholics who have mountains of credit card debt. What do they always say when they drag home shopping bags full of stuff they don't need?

"But it was all on sale!"

In other words, "I had the itch to buy something, and the store helped me feel good about it by offering everything I wanted for 40 percent off!"

A few years ago when flat-screen HD TVs were taking the electronics world by storm, I wanted one. I would gaze longingly at them in stores. I would fantasize about how good my Cardinals games would look in HD. And then I would look at the prices (remember, they were a lot more expensive in those days) and walk away slump-shouldered. But soon after, sometimes the same day, I would run into one of my friends who had one and he would say, "Man, you have got to get yourself a flat screen. Dude, they are awesome!" One time a friend even said, "You work hard. You deserve something like that for all you do."

As has been well documented in this chapter, today is Black Friday, which means that every other commercial on TV is advertising potential Christmas gifts. My six-year-old granddaughter, Alyssa, is at that age where every little girl toy seems like just the thing she needs to make her life complete. After every toy commercial she looks at me or her grandma and says, "I want that."

The other evening, after about seven or eight *I want thats*, I said, "Alyssa, you want everything." She looked at me and grinned and said, "Yes, I do."

There's always going to be someone or something around to affirm our *I want thats*. A television commercial, a friend, a 50 percent-off sale . . . they're all lined up, just waiting to help you feel good about your materialistic impulses.

WHY MATERIALISTIC PEOPLE ARE SELDOM HAPPY

The book of Ecclesiastes is basically Solomon explaining how wrong he was about happiness. He thought it would grow right along with his wealth. He believed that the more stuff he accumulated, the happier he would be. He was wrong. Right now the world is full of people who are discovering the same error in their thinking. Some are young and just starting to feel small twinges of disappointment. Others are older and suffering regret on an epic scale. So let's think about it. Why do materialistic people so often end up unhappy?

REASON #1: THEY CAN'T PREDICT THE FUTURE

Look at this little dose of common sense from Solomon in Ecclesiastes 10:8–9: "When you dig a well, you might fall in. When you demolish an old wall, you could be bitten by a snake. When you work in a quarry, stones might fall and crush you. When you chop wood, there is danger with each stroke of your ax."

So much of the acquisition of wealth depends on the anticipation of future events. Which stocks are going to soar, and which ones are going to crash? Which new products are going to catch on, and which ones are going to be quickly forgotten? Which young entrepreneurs are going to be successful, and which ones are going to be mere flashes in the pan? Which one of the companies that wants to hire me is going to thrive, and which one is going to go out of business in five years?

In this passage, Solomon is pointing out one of life's great eternal truths: you just never know what's going to happen. You go out to dig a well, thinking it to be no big deal. How hard can it be to scoop dirt? But then you fall in and break your back. Or you pick up your ax, kiss your sweetie good-bye, and tell her you'll be home for dinner with some firewood. But while you're chopping you get distracted and hack off half your foot.

Life is the greatest curveball pitcher in history.

Just when you think you have it all figured out . . . just when you think you have the perfect strategy . . . just when you think you know what company to invest in . . . just when you think you have a leg up on the competition, something happens that you weren't counting on.

Several years ago, a good friend of mine came to me all depressed. I'd never seen him in such a state. I thought his wife had died or something. It turned out he had invested a huge chunk of his life savings in a project that went belly-up. A Christian brother of his had pitched to him a "can't miss" opportunity. He told me it was his one chance to finally get ahead of the pack. He learned too late that there's no such thing as a "can't miss" opportunity, even if it is dubbed so by a Christian brother. In fact, I'll go so far as to say that if anyone ever comes to you with a "can't miss" opportunity, run as fast as you can in the other direction.

REASON #2: THEY CAN'T OUTSMART THE COMPETITION

Extremely wealthy people are often thought of as being brilliant, and sometimes they are. But brilliance is no guarantee of financial success. Albert Einstein, for example, was arguably the most intelligent man who has ever lived. Most of us have no idea what the theory of relativity is, but we know it's a big deal and that he discovered it. He also won the Nobel Prize in physics and led the way to major advances in radiation, statistical mechanics, and quantum theory. But he failed at investing. Big time. He even lost his Nobel Prize money on bonds that defaulted.

Have you heard of Mensa International? It's a society of smart people. And by smart, I mean it's only open to people who score at the 98th percentile or higher on approved IQ tests. That includes about 2 percent of the population. But over a fifteen-year period when the S&P 500 had average annual returns of 15.3 percent, the Mensa Investment Club's performance averaged a return of just 2.5 percent.[1]

Really smart people are often highly successful in everything *but* wealth management, which frustrates them half to death. They know—we all know—there's a correlation between smarts and success. Sure, character and hard work are important, but you seldom find dumb people who are highly successful, no matter how honest and hardworking they are. So it would seem to follow that smart, highly successful people would be shoo-ins to be extremely wealthy. It just isn't true. According to the *Huffington Post*, in 2010 there were 33,655 PhD recipients on food stamps.[2]

When I was twelve years old, I was the biggest kid on my Little League team. (Because my birthday is in September, I hit my twelfth birthday about six months sooner than many of the boys I played against.) As the big kid on the team, I was supposed to be the best player. One night we played a game in Allendale, Illinois, against the only team in the league that had a home run fence. Boy, was it short. I'll bet I could have stood on home plate and thrown the ball over the fence. I just knew I was going to hit two, three, or four home runs that night. In the days leading up to the game, I fantasized about how I would trot around the bases slowly to make the experience last as long as possible.

I struck out five times.

Swinging.

As I recall, I didn't even hit a foul ball.

The feeling I had that night after the game must be similar to what really smart people experience when they strike out at investing. It's that feeling of knowing you should be able to do better and wondering what went wrong.

REASON #3: THEY CAN'T RESIST TEMPTATION

Actually, none of us can resist temptation. We all give in to one sooner or later. But it's especially hard for materialistic people to say no to any temptation that involves the acquisition of stuff. The problem is that the acquisition of stuff usually brings payments, and payments bring pressure, and pressure does a number on your happiness.

A few years ago a friend of mine was blessed with a gigantic boost in his family income. He'd always talked about how, if he had money, he would do this and that. I mostly paid no attention to his ramblings, figuring he'd never make enough money to do half the things he was talking about. Well, suddenly, he did. And sure enough, he started doing all the things he said he was going to do. He bought a beautiful home and filled it with brand-new furniture. He bought a thirty-five-thousand-dollar pickup. He even bought a grill that looked like a commercial kitchen. Almost overnight he was living the life he'd always dreamed of, but he owned nothing outright. He was making payments on everything. Big payments.

Only a few months after he got everything just the way he wanted it, the economy started to slip.

And slip.

And slip.

I was recently in the neighborhood and drove by his beautiful home. It wasn't beautiful anymore. It was grown up in weeds. He apparently had to move. I don't know to where. Maybe he's somewhere living a perfectly happy life, but I doubt it. Not unless he's changed. If he hasn't, I can pretty much figure that he's somewhere talking about all the things he's going to buy if he ever gets his hands on some money.

REASON #4: THEY CAN'T ADMIT THE TRUTH

Jesus said the truth would set us free. That's particularly true when it comes to materialism. What truth am I referring to? I'll let an older, reflective Solomon tell you: "Those who love money will never have enough. How meaningless to think that wealth brings true happiness! The more you have, the more people come to help you spend it. So what good is wealth—except perhaps to watch it slip through your fingers!" (Eccl. 5:10–11).

Materialistic people tend to believe everything but the truth when it comes to money and material things. Tell them you have a "can't miss" investment opportunity and they'll fall all over themselves writing you a check. Tell them there's a new gadget that is all the rage and they'll break every speed limit in town getting to Best Buy. Tell them a rival just bought a new car and they'll be prowling the car lots as soon as they get off work. But tell them material things never bring true happiness and they'll say, "Yeah, right" and go right on chasing them as hard as they can until they're miserable. The apostle Paul said it best: "People who long to be rich fall into temptation and are trapped by many foolish and harmful desires that plunge them into ruin and destruction. For the love of money is the root of all kinds of evil. And some people, craving money, have wandered from the true faith and pierced themselves with many sorrows" (1 Tim. 6:9–10).

HOW TO OVERCOME MATERIALISM

Do you have a materialistic bent? Has reading the preceding paragraphs felt like looking into a mirror? If you're not sure (which I find hard to believe), look at your credit card balances.

Consider the clutter that surrounds you. Is your garage so full of stuff that you can't squeeze your car in?

Are you ridiculously upside down on your car because you keep buying a new one before you get the old one paid off?

Is overkill one of the overarching themes of your life? (I know a hunter who owns twenty-three guns.)

When you buy something, do you pay extra to get the elite brand name, even though the cheaper off-brand is just as good?

Do you make good money but have trouble saving?

Do you buy some things on the sly because you know they would be hard to justify?

When one of your friends buys something really cool, do you feel the urge to get one for yourself?

Do you play the lottery and fantasize about what you would buy if you won?

If you're married, do you find yourself often getting defensive toward your spouse when arguing about money?

If you do have a materialistic bent, there is good news: materialism is curable. The cure does, however, require some hard work, most of which will be done between your ears. A simple way to approach this work is to think about five trades you need to make.

TRADE #1: ACCUMULATION FOR ALLOCATION

We live in a stockpiling, collecting, hoarding culture. There are several reasons for this. One is that we fear scarcity. Hardly a week goes by that we don't hear about a shortage of something. Another reason we live in accumulation mode is to achieve status. We may not actually believe the bumper sticker that says, "Whoever dies with the most toys wins," but we do believe, and rightfully so, that most people will think better of us if we live in nice homes, drive nice cars, and have lots of stuff. And the third reason we collect and hoard is that we don't really trust God to provide for our needs. Okay, some people do, but most don't. Surveys have always shown that one of the biggest things we worry about is not having enough money, which is just as much a commentary on our faith (or lack thereof) as it is on our fear of circumstances.

Of course, none of this is new.

Two thousand years ago, Jesus told a story about a man whose barns became so full that he couldn't squeeze another thing in (Luke 12:16–21). Some people would have paused at that point and said, "Hmm, maybe I have enough. Maybe it's time to start giving to the less fortunate." But this man was a first-class hoarder, so he decided to tear down his barns and build bigger ones. Was he afraid of a coming shortage? Was he trying to elevate himself in the community? Did he not trust God? I don't know, but Jesus called him a fool.

Solomon eventually admitted that he made a mistake, too, when he was living in full accumulation mode. He said, "There is another serious problem I have seen under the sun. Hoarding riches harms the saver" (Eccl. 5:13).

The answer to this "serious problem" is to trade accumulation for allocation. In other words, to start giving, to start spreading your wealth around. And I mean in a serious way, not just dropping your pocket change into the Salvation Army bucket, but really digging deep and being extra generous. Does that sound extreme? It is, but we must understand that there's only one way to beat extreme behavior, and that's *with* extreme behavior.

An alcoholic, for example, will never kick his drinking problem by trying to cut back and drink in moderation. The only hope he has is to stop drinking completely. A porn addict will never overcome his addiction by looking at fewer dirty pictures. The only hope he has is to stop looking at dirty pictures altogether.

The same is true with materialism. It can only be defeated with extreme generosity. That's why, when Jesus was approached by a rich man who was a hoarder (Mark 10:17–27), he didn't mollycoddle him with some vague platitudes about not buying so much stuff. He flat out told the guy to sell all his possessions. That's right, *all* his possessions! Jesus knew that the way to beat extreme behavior is *with* extreme behavior. He was telling hoarders in every generation to do an about-face, to trade accumulation for allocation.

TRADE #2: SOMEDAY FOR TODAY

It's good to think about the future. The Bible extols the virtues of good planning. But materialistic people obsess over the future. Why? Because the future is when they will have acquired all the stuff they want. The dream job, the dream house, the dream car, the dream man cave, the dream vacation . . . they don't have it all yet, but someday they hope to.

It's a false hope.

The reality is that no matter how far they travel into the future, materialistic people never reach that place where they feel content enough to sit back and say, "*Someday* is finally here. I have everything I want!" Nonmaterialistic people reach that place all the time. Many of them have lived contentedly in that place for years. But materialistic people never get there because every time they acquire something they want and mark it off their list, another item comes along and takes its place.

Solomon said, "Enjoy what you have rather than desiring what you don't have" (Eccl. 6:9). In other words, trade someday for today.

TRADE #3: TODAY FOR SOMEDAY

Right now you're thinking, *Wait a minute. Isn't that the opposite of what you just said?* Yes, because now I'm going to give you the one exception to that rule. You do understand that there's almost always an exception, right? For example, you should never say never, except when you're telling someone to never say never. Got it?

Okay then, here's the one instance where focusing on someday will serve you well: when you're tempted by a get-rich-quick scheme.

Every con artist in the world knows that materialistic people make the biggest suckers. Someone offers them a chance to make a lot of money in a hurry and their little hearts (bless 'em) start going pitter-pat and they start salivating like an alley cat on his way to the dumpster behind his favorite seafood restaurant. And it doesn't have to be some kind of complicated Madoff-like Ponzi scheme. Casinos and state lotteries take millions from people who, if they would just invest money they're gambling away, would end up far richer in the long run.

Key words: In. The. Long. Run.

The problem with a lot of people today is that they want to accumulate a lifetime of wealth by the time they're forty. That, more than any other reason, is why you're always hearing about some new scam going around. The bad guys know it's easy picking out there with the world so full of materialistic people.

TRADE #4: THE BALANCE SHEET FOR THE BALANCED LIFE

I've known many workaholics. I've even been one at times. So I know how the game is played. You take time away from your family, from rest, from recreation, and from spiritual disciplines like worship, prayer, and Bible study and apply it to work. And you justify it by pointing to the balance sheet.

"We need the money."

"I need to work now while my health is good."

"I may not always have this opportunity."

"We've got college educations to pay for."

Yada, yada, yada.

There's no end to the important-sounding rationalizations materialistic people use to justify their imbalanced lives. They think that by making it a balance sheet issue, they will eliminate resistance. After all, what wife in her right mind wouldn't want to be financially secure and have her children's college educations paid for? She may wish her husband didn't work so much, but with those college educations looming on the horizon like storm clouds, she's not going to say much, which allows her husband to continue being a workaholic without resistance.

The problem is that materialism/workaholism does not guarantee financial security, let alone happiness. To hear workaholics talk, you'd think it does. But look around. The world is full of broke workaholics.

And divorced workaholics.

And stressed-out workaholics.

And unhappy workaholics.

And dead workaholics.

Trading the balance sheet for a balanced life is huge. It will positively affect your health, your relationships, and your spiritual development. And here's a surprise . . . it likely won't diminish your productivity! More and more people are waking up to the fact that with so many tools at our disposal nowadays (such as computer conferencing), it's possible for almost everyone to get more done in less time.

TRADE #5: MONEY FOR GOD

Ultimately it comes down to what Jesus said in Matthew 6:24: "No one can serve two masters. For you will hate one and love the other; you will be devoted to one and despise the other. You cannot serve both God and money."

No one illustrates this better than Solomon. The more he chased wealth and possessions, the further he drifted from God. It's the reason why God firmly stated that a king should not accumulate horses and gold. He knew what would happen.

In my almost four decades of ministry, I've met wealthy people who were godly, but I can honestly say that I've never met a truly godly person who was frantically chasing wealth. I've met wealth chasers who attended church and wanted me to think they were godly. Perhaps they were also trying to convince themselves that they were godly. But I could always see plenty of evidence to the contrary.

Jesus was right. You can't serve both God and money.

As I was researching this chapter, I made a startling discovery. Before I state it, understand that I am speaking in general terms. You will be able to find isolated verses here and there that go against the flow of what I'm about to say, but generally, what I'm saying is true. (If you doubt me, check for yourself.)

In the Old Testament, wealth and prosperity are tied to God's blessing. Starting with Abraham (Gen. 13:2), the patriarchs were all wealthy, as were David and Solomon. Even common people thought in terms of wealth being a by-product of one's faithfulness to God. For example, consider this passage, which is typical of many in the Old Testament:

> May our sons flourish in their youth
>   like well-nurtured plants.
> May our daughters be like graceful pillars,
>   carved to beautify a palace.
> May our barns be filled
>   with crops of every kind.

May the flocks in our fields multiply by the thousands,
    even tens of thousands,
    and may our oxen be loaded down with produce.
May there be no enemy breaking through our walls,
    no going into captivity,
    no cries of alarm in our town squares.
Yes, joyful are those who live like this!
    Joyful indeed are those whose God is the LORD. (Ps. 144:12–15)

But in the New Testament, the tone is quite different. In fact, of the almost ninety references to prosperity, all but two appear in the Old Testament. In the New Testament, the poor are held up as models of spirituality and warnings are given to those who are wealthy. For example, in Luke's recitation of the Beatitudes, Jesus said:

"God blesses you who are poor,
    for the Kingdom of God is yours.
God blesses you who are hungry now,
    for you will be satisfied.
God blesses you who weep now,
    for in due time you will laugh." (6:20–21)

Then, just three verses later, Jesus added: "What sorrow awaits you who are rich, for you have your only happiness now " (v. 24).

Allow me to venture a guess as to what's behind this change in tone.

It is an answer to the change that had occurred in man's thinking.

In the Old Testament, the common man felt rich if he had a nice family, a few head of cattle, and a roof over his head. However, as civilization developed, cities were built, commerce was expanded, businesses were launched, and serious amounts of money started changing hands, not just between kings, as was primarily the case in

Solomon's time, but between ordinary people. The result was that a hardworking man with a good head on his shoulders could get ahead financially, a realization that triggered a materialistic hunger in ordinary folks that was not unlike what people experienced during the gold rush of the 1800s. When Paul wrote about those "who long to be rich" (1 Tim. 6:9), he was addressing this hunger.

Today, we live in a culture that has advanced light-years beyond even what Paul was seeing when he wrote to Timothy. For the price of a lottery ticket, paupers can skyrocket to unfathomable riches. With the pull of a lever on a slot machine or a well-played hand of cards or a few well-chosen investments, people can embrace a lifestyle they once only dreamed of, which means that we, more than any generation in history, need to be on guard against materialism.

I challenge you to examine yourself in the light of what you've just read. Your drinking cups may not be made of gold, but if your workweek is longer than forty-five hours, your house is crammed full of stuff, your credit cards are maxed out, and you can still think of things you want, it's almost a certainty that you've been seduced.

WAKE-UP CALL №8

YOU KNOW YOU'RE BEING SEDUCED WHEN THERE ARE A THOUSAND WOMEN LINED UP OUTSIDE YOUR BATHROOM

AND NOW FOR THE WOMEN.

They are the first thing most people think about when Solomon is mentioned. Okay, they're the first thing most *guys* think about. Sure, we're impressed with the man's wealth and wisdom. Who wouldn't be? But it's the harem that causes our craniums to crumble. Maybe it's because most of us have a hard time keeping *one* woman happy. The thought of trying to deal with a thousand is, well, let me put it this way: I'd rather swab the deck of the *Queen Mary* with a toothbrush than try to keep a thousand women happy.

And yet, be honest: don't you wonder what it must have been like?

If Solomon was a typical, sex-loving male, he literally could have had it anytime he wanted it. And always with a raving beauty.

Think about that.

The excuse, "Sorry, honey, I have a headache," would have never bothered Solomon too much because there was always another centerfold-quality female waiting in the wings.

"But wait a minute," you say. "Surely, they couldn't have *all* been gorgeous."

I wouldn't be too sure. In Ecclesiastes 2:8, Solomon makes reference to "many beautiful concubines." Considering his penchant for getting whatever he wanted, I suspect there were a lot of homecoming queens in the bunch and very few Miss Congenialities. But for the sake of discussion, let's say only half of them were beautiful. That's still five hundred gorgeous women at your beck and call.

Five. Hundred. Gorgeous. Women.

To appreciate this number, think about the Miss America pageant, where there are fifty of the most beautiful women in the United States on the stage. Blondes, brunettes, and redheads, all with movie star looks.

Now multiply by ten.

By *ten.*

And picture them all waiting to please you.

See what I mean?

When considering Solomon's women, we come to the most mind-bending part of the story. It's impossible to fathom what he experienced in the romantic/sexual area of his life because we have no point of reference. We're like a panhandler trying to understand what it's like to be a millionaire. Nevertheless, we will soldier on because this is a critical aspect of Solomon's saga, the point at which we come to some of the darkest aspects of his seduction— and some of the most powerful lessons for modern men.

HAREM BUILDING, 900 BC

Solomon was very goal-oriented. You can see it in his political strategies, business deals, and building projects. However, I doubt that he ever contemplated amassing such a ridiculously large harem. I just can't see him with his generals and advisors, saying, "And while we're building this temple, let's also see how many good-looking women we can talk into marrying me." Nevertheless, it happened. There came a day when Solomon had enough wives and concubines to make twenty-seven sets of Radio City Music Hall Rockettes.

I believe three factors played a part in this stockpiling of women.

FACTOR #1: POLITICS

Solomon's first wife came to him in the alliance he made with the king of Egypt (1 Kings 3:1). How many others were acquired the same way? We don't know, but likely quite a few. In those days, kings liked to swap daughters as a way of fostering good relations between their countries. And, from a purely secular perspective, why not? If I'm a king, I have to figure that the ruler of the kingdom next door will be less likely to launch an attack against me if he knows his own flesh and blood is living in my palace.

FACTOR #2: PRIDE

As I pointed out in chapter 3, when Solomon first became king, he was the model of humility. In 1 Kings 3:7–9, he said, "I am like a little child who doesn't know his way around. And here I am in the midst of your own chosen people, a nation so great and numerous they cannot be counted! Give me an understanding heart so that I can govern your people well and know the difference between right and wrong. For who by himself is able to govern this great people of yours?"

But it wasn't long before his ego began to grow.

And grow.

And grow.

Until, eventually, Solomon was so full of himself that he wanted to be number one in everything.

Temples? Check.

Palaces? Check.

Fancy thrones? Check.

Solid gold utensils? Check.

Horses? Check.

Wives? Check.

Solomon became the George Steinbrenner of the ancient world. (Steinbrenner, for you non-baseball fans, was the prideful owner of the New York Yankees during many of their glory years. He had unfathomably deep pockets and spared no expense in seeing to it that the Yanks took a backseat to no other organization.)

It wouldn't surprise me if Solomon sent spies out to find out what other kings had—the sizes of their palaces, thrones, harems—and then made sure his were bigger.

FACTOR #3: PASSION

This is where the mind starts to bend. Politics and pride we can understand. But the Bible says Solomon actually loved these women (1 Kings 11:1–2). I get that he could love having the biggest harem of all his king buddies. I get that he could love always having a beautiful woman at his beck and call. I get that he could love a few of the women who happened to be his favorites. But the Bible says he loved *many* of these women. If you're running a country and involved in as many building projects as Solomon was, how do you have time to even get to know many of these women, let alone love them?

It's obvious that the love Solomon had for these women was not as deep or as meaningful as what a devoted, monogamous couple would share. And yet we cannot deny that, to him, this harem was more than a status symbol, more than mere amusement, more than just a way to find sexual fulfillment. On some level, Solomon gave his heart to these women, which explains why he built altars to their foreign gods and began worshipping those gods himself. It was a stunning and almost pathetic attempt to please them. Could there be a more obvious sign that Solomon was at last completely seduced?

Granted, Solomon wasn't the first or the last man to let the love of a woman (or women) turn him into a fool. But he may be the most surprising, considering that he warned about the dangers of sexual sin in his writing. In the fifth, sixth, and seventh chapters of Proverbs, Solomon offers lengthy and very descriptive warnings to men not to allow themselves to be sexually seduced. Further, he speaks of the value of having a single wife and of letting her be "a fountain of blessing for you" (Prov. 5:18). Once again, Solomon knew the right thing to do, but didn't do it.

A WORLD OF ILLUSION

I'm an avid fiction reader. I like a wide range of genres, including thrillers, mysteries, and sprawling historical epics. If there's one thing a book blurb can say about the plot of a novel that will hook me every time, it's this: "Nothing is what it seems." I love books that are full of surprises, where the good guy turns out to be the bad guy, or the character you think is dead is really alive. I am a complete sucker for an unexpected plot twist.

Let me clarify: in *fiction* I like surprises.

I don't like them at all in real life. I absolutely hate it when I discover that something I thought was true isn't true at all. In my experience, when that realization hits, there's usually some pain involved and perhaps even some broken pieces to pick up.

I'm pretty sure that no one who reads this book is ever going to have a thousand wives and mistresses like Solomon, but I do anticipate that many will be tangled up in illicit romantic relationships, or at least may be heading in that direction. That's why I want to spend the rest of this chapter explaining why the world of sexual sin is truly the ultimate world of illusion. Men (and women) who choose this path discover sooner or later that they walked into a dimension where nothing is what it seems. Consider these ten illusions and take them as a dire warning.

ILLUSION #1: THAT WHICH SEEMS HARMLESS IS ACTUALLY DANGEROUS

What seems harmless?

Married men and women flirting with people other than their spouses.

They do it all the time. Sometimes they do it with body language, sometimes with seemingly casual, yet not-so-innocent touches, sometimes with suggestive comments, and sometimes just with a look. Sometimes they do it openly and sometimes on the sly. And often it's very calculated. A man, for example, when he knows he's going to be seeing the woman he's attracted to, might choose a certain cologne while a woman might shop for an outfit that flatters her figure and just happens to be his favorite color.

Challenge a flirtatious person and you'll likely get one of the following two responses:

"Who, me? I'm not flirtatious. I'm just outgoing and friendly!"

Or . . .

"I know I'm a flirt, but it's all in fun. I'd never actually do anything."

You want to know how dumb that last statement is? Consider this: every illicit sexual relationship in the history of the world started with flirting. That's right—every single one!

What if you knew that every single car accident in the history of the world involved a Ford? Would you buy one? Of course not. You'd most likely say, "No Fords for me—they're too dangerous!" Or what if every single plane crash involved the same airline? Would you book a flight on that airline or choose a different one? Flirtation is the starting point for *every* illicit sexual relationship. Over the years I've talked to countless people who've had affairs. I've asked them to tell me how the relationship got started and, even though the details differ slightly, the basic story is always the same: innocent flirting led to something more. And yes, they almost always use the word *innocent* when talking about the initial stages of the relationship. They often say, "We were just friends. We never intended for anything to happen." They believed that what they were doing was harmless, but it was an illusion.

Right now, if you're involved in a flirtatious relationship with someone who is not your spouse, you need to back off. You can plead your case all day long, that it's all totally innocent, that you have no illicit intent, and maybe that's true. But you cannot deny you are traveling a road that is littered with the corpses of people who used to say the same thing. Solomon said of the seductive woman, "Don't let her coy glances seduce you" (Prov. 6:25). And again, "A prudent person foresees danger and takes precautions. The simpleton goes blindly on and suffers the consequences" (Prov. 22:3).

ILLUSION #2: THAT WHICH SEEMS PERFECT IS ACTUALLY FLAWED

What seems perfect?

Why, the other woman, of course!

Your wife nags you, while the other woman praises you.

Your wife rolls her eyes at your jokes, while the other woman practically falls down laughing at every witty little thing you say.

Your wife obsesses over the kids and the finances and the laundry, while the other woman is interested in only you.

Your wife wears frumpy clothes, while the other woman is always dressed to the nines and smelling like a field of lilacs.

Your wife has a ho-hum attitude toward sex, while the other woman is as interested in it as you are.

Your wife makes you feel trapped, while the other woman fires up your dreams and makes you believe life offers a myriad of wonderful possibilities.

And it's all a big fat lie.

Here's the truth: that other woman who seems so perfect is deeply flawed or she wouldn't be in a relationship with you, a married man!

Not long ago a guy who was embroiled in an extramarital affair talked with me. He said, "I know it's crazy, but I really believe she [the other woman] is my soul mate."

I said, "You're right. It's crazy."

He bristled.

I stared at him.

He said, "Why do you say it's crazy?"

I said, "I was just agreeing with you. You're the one who said it was crazy."

He blinked and looked confused. Finally, he said, "But . . . but she seems so perfect for me."

I said, "So did your wife when you married her."

He blinked again, searching for something to say.

Can we just be honest here? Any man or woman who would engage in an illicit sexual affair has serious issues, possibly far more serious than you might imagine. (Do the words "fatal attraction" mean anything to you?) I'm not saying such a person is doomed or hopeless or anything of the sort. But I am saying that feeling you have that your paramour is the most perfect human being to ever put toe to turf is ridiculous. Why do you think most men who get busted in affairs go crawling back to their wives, begging for mercy and proclaiming themselves utter fools?

ILLUSION #3: THAT WHICH EXCITES YOU ACTUALLY DEADENS YOU

What excites you?

Your fantasies.

The biggest part of an illicit relationship is played out between your ears. This is especially true in the flirting stage. Before the sneaking around and the sex begin, your mind is a tornado of possibilities. A suggestive comment is made and suddenly your heart kicks up about ten beats per minute as you ponder all sorts of delicious possibilities. Then, when you move beyond the flirting stage to the sex and the sneaking around, your fantasies explode. No longer are you wondering what she would look like naked; you're now thinking about how wonderful it would be if you two could live together forever in what you just know would be a sort of never-ending honeymoon. You're talking about where you'd like to live and how you'd spend your weekends and all the things that would be different from your current situation.

I've heard men in the middle of this experience say, "I've never felt more alive!" The truth is, they've never been more dead. Proverbs 21:16 says it best: "The person who strays from common sense will end up in the company of the dead."

He'll be dead to the truth about the relationship.

Dead to the reality of his spiritual condition.

Dead to the trouble he's making for himself.

Dead to the damage he's doing to his loved ones.

Dead to the promptings of the Holy Spirit.

Not surprisingly, I hear a lot of repentant adulterers talk about their past affairs in terms that sound as though they could be talking about death:

"I went brain dead."

"I lost touch with reality."

"I was really out of it."

But in the beginning, when the fantasies were flying, they felt so alive and excited.

ILLUSION #4: THAT WHICH SEEMS TO JUSTIFY ACTUALLY CONDEMNS

What seems to justify your actions?

A laundry list of rationalizations.

I can't count the times I've sat and listened to men try to explain why *their* actions should be viewed differently than your run-of-the-mill cheater. And, regardless of the age of the individual or the circumstances, the excuses are always the same:

"My wife doesn't understand me."

"I tried for years to be a good husband."

"My wife just isn't the same person I married."

"I can't help how I feel."

"I wasn't looking for a relationship like this."

"God brought this woman into my life."

"We just seem so perfect for each other."

"I know God doesn't want me to be unhappy."

I am always amazed at the passion with which people say these ridiculous things. I've seen guys slide up on the edge of their seats, get red in the face, raise their voices, and use grandiose hand gestures, almost as if they were preaching. I guess it shouldn't be surprising. People who know they're wrong are typically desperate to make things appear different than they really are, and if you don't have truth on your side, it makes sense to go for emotion.

Proverbs 12:2 says, "The LORD approves of those who are good, but he condemns those who plan wickedness." Look at that last phrase: "those who plan wickedness." Isn't that what you're doing when you manufacture excuses to justify your sin? Aren't you laying the groundwork for continuing on in that sin? Aren't you planning more wickedness?

Not long ago I was talking to a woman at our church when one of her offspring was brought to her, looking quite sheepish and guilty. The mom was told what had happened and looked to the child for a confession and an apology. Instead, the kid started making excuses. I love how the mom reacted. She held up her hand like a traffic cop and said, "Stop right there and think about something before you say another word. With every excuse you make, you're getting yourself into more trouble. Now, go ahead." The kid, momentarily bewildered, finally hung his head and admitted his guilt. I think what that mom said to her son is what God would say to excuse-making cheaters.

ILLUSION #5: THAT WHICH SEEMS TO LIBERATE ACTUALLY ENSLAVES

What liberates?

Money.

Guys who have money find it much easier to carry on a secret affair. They can rent hotel rooms on the sly, purchase extra cell phones that their wives don't know about, or secretly fly their paramours to the cities they happen to be traveling to for business. If you recall, Tiger Woods had access to women and amenities that no hourly-wage employee would have ever been able to afford. Yes, money buys everything from perks to silence. Tiger had been carrying on his outrageous lifestyle for years. We might never have heard about it if he hadn't run over a fire hydrant.

But while money may liberate a man from the logistical constraints many poorer souls have to contend with, it has an epic downside, as Tiger Woods I'm sure would agree. It lures you deeper and deeper into your sin, making you more of a slave to the beast that is inevitably going to destroy you. How does it lure you deeper into your sin? By fixing first one problem and then another.

Need a place to rendezvous?

Rent a hotel room.

Need to keep the hotel clerk quiet?

Give him a generous tip.

Need to keep your wife out of your phone?

Buy another one with a number she doesn't know about.

Need your secretary's help keeping the affair a secret?

Give her a nice raise.

Need to convince your fussy lover that you really care?

Buy her a diamond bracelet.

If you buy your way out of enough problems, you eventually start thinking you can buy your way out of every problem. From that point on, the money option will be the first thing that comes to your mind when the relationship creates tension. Instead of considering repentance and confession, you'll ask yourself how much money it will take to fix things. At that point, no matter how deep your pockets are, you're anything but free. You're a slave.

ILLUSION #6: THAT WHICH YOU THOUGHT WOULD FACILITATE YOUR FUN ACTUALLY FACILITATES YOUR DOOM

What facilitates your fun?

Technology.

Just ask Anthony Weiner, a seven-term congressman.

Or Brett Favre, a soon-to-be NFL Hall of Famer.

Or Tiger Woods, at one time the world's greatest golfer.

Or Greg Oden, an NBA first-round draft pick.

Or John Ensign, a former senator from Nevada.

All of these guys' sexual shenanigans were exposed, in part, because of the way they used their cell phones. Pictures and text messages that were wildly inappropriate brought them fun and excitement, but not half as much fun and excitement as trouble. At the very least they were embarrassed; at the worst (Weiner and Ensign) they lost their careers.

Technology is a blessing to mankind, but it can spell trouble for people who lack self-discipline. Chat rooms, e-mails, text messages, tweets, and digital pictures are just a few of the technological land mines that cheaters often step on.

ILLUSION #7: THAT WHICH SEEMS CERTAIN IS ACTUALLY THE LONGEST OF LONG SHOTS

What seems certain?

Fulfillment.

The cheating man senses that he's finally found what he's been looking for his whole life: an attractive woman who understands him, admires him, believes in him, and doesn't act as though sex is about as exciting as watching C-SPAN reruns. Of course, he felt the same way when he was dating his wife, but (to his way of thinking) that's apples and oranges. He was young then. Now he's more mature and understands his needs and the kind of woman it takes to meet them.

Did you like the C-SPAN line I just rolled out?

Clever, huh?

But in the interest of full disclosure, I have to admit that I stole it. It was actually said to me by a man who was explaining why he felt his wildest dreams were finally coming true with a woman who was not his wife. In the interest of full disclosure, I should tell you that same man eventually went back to his wife and begged her to forgive him. Seems the ultimate fulfillment of his hopes and dreams wasn't quite as certain as he thought.

I'm not going to deny that a few adulterers end up staying with their lovers and finding some measure of happiness, but the percentage is very small. Most of the time the illicit relationship that first seems like Utopia gradually morphs into a toxic waste dump. Both men and women eventually go running from the affair and, as often as not, end up hating each other. You may have a slightly better chance of finding fulfillment in an affair than you do of winning the lottery, but not by much.

ILLUSION #8: THAT WHICH SEEMS MEANINGFUL IS MEANINGLESS

What seems meaningful during an affair?

A deeper spiritual commitment.

I know it sounds silly, but hear me out. I've seen it again and again. People with religious upbringing or even a current connection to the church will often find ways to spiritualize their sexual sin. It's more than just saying, "I believe God brought this person into my life" or "I know God doesn't want me to be unhappy." It's an attempt to establish the affair as a tool God is using to bring spiritual growth.

Years ago, I spoke with a man who was involved in an extramarital relationship. He said something very close to this: "Mark, I know you think what we're doing is wrong, but believe me when I tell you God is using the relationship to his glory. We've actually been praying and reading the Bible together." He was talking about himself and his lover.

I said, "No kidding? When you pray, what do you pray about?"

He said, "We just pray that God will do what he wants with our relationship. If he doesn't want us to be together, then we say, 'Break us up, Lord.' But since we've been praying that prayer, he hasn't broken us up. In fact, we've only fallen deeper in love."

I wonder if David didn't engage in this kind of broken thinking. Most scholars believe it was about a year from the time he began his affair with Bathsheba until the prophet Nathan showed up to confront him about his sin. During that year, David would have been worshipping and offering sacrifices to God. How did he reconcile that in his mind? How did he rationalize it to his associates? I assume from the fact that he didn't repent during that twelve-month period that he found ways to convince himself that God was smiling on him.

A good verse for David or anyone else who tries to fit sexual sin comfortably into his relationship with God is Isaiah 29:13. God said, "These people say they are mine. They honor me with their lips, but their hearts are far from me."

ILLUSION #9: THAT WHICH SEEMS SO TERRIFYING OFFERS RELIEF

What terrifies?

The idea of getting caught.

One man's experience in sexual sin might vary from another's, depending on the details. But the one thing virtually all cheating men share is the fear of getting busted.

In 2012, General David Petraeus was busted for an affair he had with his biographer. The morning after it was first reported, I saw an article online that listed famous men who had been caught cheating on their wives. (It always amazes me how quickly journalists come up with this stuff.) The list was filled with politicians, athletes, CEOs, and entertainers. Some of them had been able to move on with their careers, but many were ruined professionally and lost their marriages to boot. I had a repentant cheater tell me one time that, while he was involved in the illicit relationship, he used to hate hearing news stories about guys getting caught cheating on their wives. He said he would almost always have what felt like a panic attack. Sometimes after watching such a news report, he would have nightmares.

At the same time, I've heard guys who got caught say it was the best thing that ever happened to them. Yes, they were terrified of it before it happened and took extreme measures to avoid exposure, but after the fact they admitted that it was the only thing that could've broken them out of the prison in which they found themselves.

ILLUSION #10: THAT WHICH SEEMS EASY IS HARD

What seems easy?

Quitting.

A man who is being drawn into a questionable relationship tells himself that everything is okay because he can quit anytime he wants. "If I see that things are getting out of control, I'll just pull the plug," he tells himself. And more than likely, he means it. But when things begin getting out of control, when lines are crossed and forbidden territory is entered, he finds the quitting option to be far more complicated than he thought it would be.

First, he finds it complicated by his own feelings. Yes, he knows he needs to quit—and maybe deep down he wants to—but at the same time, he's never known such excitement! How can he walk away from this woman who gives him so much pleasure?

Second, he finds quitting complicated by the potential fallout. What will the woman's response be if he ends the relationship? He can explain from here to Christmas how it's the right thing to do, but will she agree? Will she go gently into that good night (to paraphrase Dylan Thomas), or will she morph into Glenn Close's character from *Fatal Attraction*? I've had a number of guys tell me that they were afraid to carry on with an affair but were even more afraid to quit.

Third, he may well find quitting complicated by circumstances. What if the person he's in the illicit relationship with is a family friend, a coworker, or a boss? Will cutting the cord create so much awkwardness that perceptive family members or colleagues will figure out what was going on? And if that were the case, would it defeat the purpose of quitting?

"I can quit anytime I want," sounds really good when you're

trying to justify your actions. But quitting is easier said than done.

As I finish up this chapter, a couple I know and love is separating because of an adulterous relationship. I'm praying that the marriage can be saved, but at this point it's not looking good. When I spoke to the party who committed the sin, this was a statement I heard: "It's amazing to me how different things looked before and after we crossed the line. Before, I kept thinking I had everything under control and it was all okay. After, I thought, *Oh my gosh! What was I thinking?*" That statement gave me the idea to work up this list of all the illusions involved in an illicit romantic relationship, the things that look different before than they do after.

I get the feeling that Solomon also had an oh-my-gosh-what-was-I-thinking moment. After talking about his many accomplishments, including the building of his championship harem, he said, "It was all so meaningless—like chasing the wind" (Eccl. 2:11).

If you're involved in an inappropriate relationship, whether it's just in the flirting stage or already in the sneaking-around-and-having-sex stage, you need to end it. (Remember, Jesus made it clear in Matthew 5:28 that adultery need not involve physical contact.) If you don't end it, bad things are going to happen, not just to you, but to the people you love and who do not deserve to be hurt. Proverbs 6:27–28 says, "Can a man scoop a flame into his lap and not have his clothes catch on fire? Can he walk on hot coals and not blister his feet?"

In 1 Corinthians 6:18, Paul said, "Run from sexual sin!" You know what I find so interesting about that verse? The answer to one of the most life-destroying sins known to man is so simple it can be stated in four little words, the longest of which has only six letters.

We're not talking brain surgery here.

Run.

From.

Sexual.

Sin.

Don't think about it, study it, debate it, analyze it, research it, seek counsel about it, or even pray about. Just run from it!

Proverbs 5:21 says, "For the LORD sees clearly what a man does, examining every path he takes." That means God knows all about what you're up to (even if no one else does) and is, for the moment, waiting to see what you're going to do.

It's your move.

WAKE-UP CALL №9

YOU KNOW YOU'RE BEING SEDUCED WHEN THE THRONE OF YOUR HEART GOES FROM BEING A CHAIR TO A SOFA TO A SECTIONAL

OF ALL THE SAD WORDS WE'VE READ ABOUT SOLOMON UP TO THIS point, none are sadder than the ones we come to now:

> Now King Solomon loved many foreign women. Besides Pharaoh's daughter, he married women from Moab, Ammon, Edom, Sidon, and from among the Hittites. The Lord had clearly instructed the people of Israel, "You must not marry them, because they will turn your hearts to their gods." Yet Solomon insisted on loving them anyway. He had 700 wives of royal birth and 300 concubines. And in fact, they did turn his heart away from the Lord.
>
> In Solomon's old age, they turned his heart to worship other gods instead of being completely faithful to the Lord his God, as his father, David, had been. Solomon worshiped Ashtoreth, the goddess of the Sidonians, and Molech, the detestable god of the Ammonites. In this way, Solomon did

what was evil in the LORD's sight; he refused to follow the LORD completely, as his father, David, had done.

On the Mount of Olives, east of Jerusalem, he even built a pagan shrine for Chemosh, the detestable god of Moab, and another for Molech, the detestable god of the Ammonites. Solomon built such shrines for all his foreign wives to use for burning incense and sacrificing to their gods. (1 Kings 11:1–8)

That loud crash you just heard was Solomon hitting rock bottom.

Most scholars agree that, of all the bad things Solomon did, nothing was worse than breaking the first and second of the Ten Commandments, which many people consider to be just one commandment. In case it's been awhile, here they are:

"I am the LORD your God, who rescued you from the land of Egypt, the place of your slavery.

"You must not have any other god but me.

"You must not make for yourself an idol of any kind or an image of anything in the heavens or on the earth or in the sea. You must not bow down to them or worship them, for I, the LORD your God, am a jealous God who will not tolerate your affection for any other gods." (Ex. 20:1–5)

The sentence that chills me is the last one, where God says he will not tolerate our affection for any other gods. It's the ambiguity that I find disconcerting, the fact that God doesn't say *what* he will do, only that he won't tolerate our flirting with other gods. Basically, he's saying to his people, "If you violate this command, you will be sorry."

Twelve chapters after these words were delivered, the Israelites found out how sorry.

Moses had gone up Mt. Sinai to meet with God and would eventually come down with the stone tablets bearing the Ten Commandments. In the meantime, Aaron and the people were at the bottom of the mountain waiting.

And waiting.

And waiting.

We don't know how long they expected Moses to be gone, but we know he was gone longer than they expected. If you've ever gone to the ER, you know that prolonged waiting can make you antsy, and antsy people have been known to do some crazy things. In this case, the antsy Israelites, with Aaron's approval, gathered up their gold jewelry, melted it down, and molded it into the shape of a calf.

When confronted by Moses, Aaron's explanation took the concept of the lame excuse to new heights:

"Don't get so upset, my lord," Aaron replied. "You yourself know how evil these people are. They said to me, 'Make us gods who will lead us. We don't know what happened to this fellow Moses, who brought us here from the land of Egypt.' So I told them, 'Whoever has gold jewelry, take it off.' When they brought it to me, I simply threw it into the fire—and out came this calf!" (Ex. 32:22–24)

Imagine a teenager getting caught drinking one of his father's beers. Aaron's excuse to Moses is comparable to the teenager telling his dad, "All I did was open the refrigerator door and this beer jumped right into my hand!" Even the first kid who ever said, "The dog ate my homework" thinks Aaron's excuse was pathetic. Needless to say, Moses wasn't amused. More significantly, neither was God.

What happened next is chilling.

Moses stood at the entrance of the camp and called for everyone who was on God's side to gather round. It was the Levites who emerged from among the people and approached Moses. He said to them: "This is what the LORD, the God of Israel, says: Each of you, take your swords and go back and forth from one end of the camp to the other. Kill everyone—even your brothers, friends, and neighbors" (Ex. 32:27).

The Bible doesn't say so, but I feel like there must have been a question or two at that point, something along the order of, "Moses, are you sure? Is it possible that you misunderstood the Lord?" Either way, the next verse says: "The Levites obeyed Moses' command, and about 3,000 people died that day" (v. 28).

Oh, but God wasn't finished.

The next day, Moses, still reeling from the slaughter of three thousand of his countrymen (and perhaps sensing that God wasn't finished), approached the Lord on behalf of the people, asking him to forgive them. And if he wouldn't forgive them, to condemn him, Moses, as well. God shot down that idea and came up with a horrifying one of his own: "The LORD replied to Moses, 'No, I will erase the name of everyone who has sinned against me. Now go, lead the people to the place I told you about. Look! My angel will lead the way before you. And when I come to call the people to account, I will certainly hold them responsible for their sins'" (vv. 33–34).

And how did he hold them responsible? "Then the LORD sent a great plague upon the people because they had worshiped the calf Aaron had made" (v. 35).

The point of this little history lesson is to impress upon you how much God hates idolatry. And remember, Solomon would have known all about what happened at Mt. Sinai. In the same way we are taught about the Pilgrims or the signing of the Constitution, Solomon would have been taught what happened when God's law was first given to the people. It is a testimony to the thoroughness of Solomon's seduction that he could worship and build shrines to false gods, apparently without any hesitation.

WHY DOES GOD HATE IDOLATRY SO MUCH?

Just about every time I teach the golden calf story, a number of people express some disappointment in God. Surely, he overreacted. Why would he order the Levites to kill their friends and family members over a stupid statue and not issue the same punishment against, say, the sin of grumbling, which the Israelites did constantly and which truly threatened to undermine Moses' authority and derail God's plan? I remember one guy who said, "I mean, it's a *statue*, for crying out loud. It can't do anything! It's not like God suddenly had a competitor."

If similar thoughts are running through your mind right now, let me offer four reasons why God hates idolatry so much.

REASON #1: GOD HATES IDOLATRY BECAUSE IT IS DUMB

How dumb is it?

Let me put it this way. My six-year-old granddaughter plays with dolls. Sometimes she drags me into her imaginary world where I play the father or the storekeeper or the babysitter or whatever role her imagination invents for me. She holds the dolls, cuddles the dolls, talks to the dolls, and expects me to do the same. But not for one second does she think the dolls are real. If you tried to suggest to her that they were, she'd look at you like you were crazy. Even a child whose brain is about one-fourth developed knows it's stupid to treat an inanimate object like it's real.

The Bible also speaks of the absurdity of treating an inanimate object like a real person. Isaiah 44:19 says: "The person who made the idol never stops to reflect, 'Why, it's just a block of wood! I burned half of it for heat and used it to bake my bread and roast my meat. How can the rest of it be a god? Should I bow down to worship a piece of wood?'"

And then there's Habakkuk 2:18: "What good is an idol carved by man, or a cast image that deceives you? How foolish to trust in your own creation—a god that can't even talk!"

God does not insist that we all become valedictorian candidates, but even Solomon acknowledged that he takes no pleasure in fools (Eccl. 5:4). And what could be more foolish than treating a block of wood like it's a real person?

REASON #2: GOD HATES IDOLATRY BECAUSE IT IS DEMONIC

Because idols are inanimate objects, it's tempting to toss their significance aside with eye rolls and sarcastic comments. The apostle Paul, for one, didn't do that. In 1 Corinthians 10 he was reminding his readers of the sins of the Israelites during the wilderness years. He mentioned what he called "pagan revelry," sexual immorality, and idolatry. Read carefully what he said in verses 19–20: "What am I trying to say? Am I saying that food offered to idols has some significance, or that idols are real gods? No, not at all. I am saying that these sacrifices are offered to demons, not to God. And I don't want you to participate with demons."

A biblical idol may indeed be nothing more than a lifeless block of wood. But "lifeless" and "harmless" are two different things. A pill is lifeless, but if you read the list of potential side effects that comes with your prescription, you'll understand that it's not harmless. Likewise, an idol is an inanimate object, but it's also a bridge to and from Satan's lair. It opens your mind to the "evil rulers and authorities of the unseen world" (Eph. 6:12).

In 1936, Finnish army captain Kaarlo Tuurna invented

the satchel charge. It was a small shoulder bag that carried the components necessary to blow up a railway, bunker, armored vehicle, or bridge. These components included either dynamite or C-4 plastic explosive, along with a triggering mechanism. From World War II through the Vietnam War, the satchel charge saved countless lives, often by blowing up a bridge and isolating the enemy. Idolatry is one of many bridges that our spiritual enemy uses to access our hearts and minds and that needs to be blown up.

REASON #3: GOD HATES IDOLATRY BECAUSE IT IS PROGRESSIVE

It's rare that you find a reference to just one idol in Scripture. In fact, about four out of five times the word *idol* appears in Scripture, it's plural. For example, Rachel didn't have an idol in her possession; she had a sackful of them (Gen. 31:34). When Asa came to power in 1 Kings 15, we're told he "got rid of all the idols his ancestors had made" (v. 12). In the time of Jeremiah, God said, "O Israel . . . if you wanted to return to me, you could. You could throw away your detestable idols and stray away no more" (Jer. 4:1). Even hundreds of years later in the New Testament, when Paul entered Athens he was "deeply troubled by all the idols he saw everywhere in the city" (Acts 17:16).

If you believe in even one false god, it's inevitable that you're going to end up with many idols in your collection. It just wouldn't make sense to risk angering a god by excluding him from your worship rituals. Or in Solomon's case, it wouldn't make sense to risk angering one of your wives by not including her idol among those you've begun to worship.

REASON #4: GOD HATES IDOLATRY BECAUSE IT IS CONTAGIOUS

Long before Solomon caught the idolatry bug, Moses warned the Israelites that it is contagious in Deuteronomy 7:1–4:

"When the LORD your God brings you into the land you are entering to possess and drives out before you many nations— the Hittites, Girgashites, Amorites, Canaanites, Perizzites, Hivites and Jebusites, seven nations larger and stronger than you—and when the LORD your God has delivered them over to you and you have defeated them, then you must destroy them totally. Make no treaty with them, and show them no mercy. Do not intermarry with them. Do not give your daughters to their sons or take their daughters for your sons, *for they will turn your sons away from following me to serve other gods*, and the LORD's anger will burn against you and will quickly destroy you. (NIV, author's emphasis)

There are several Bible proofs that idolatry is contagious. One is the speed with which the golden calf idea spread throughout the Israelites' camp in Exodus 32. Somebody thought of it and suddenly thousands of people were demanding it.

Then there is the simple fact that so many prominent worshippers of the true God (in addition to Solomon) were guilty of it, including Rachel (Gen. 31:33–35), Gideon (Judg. 8:22–27), Micah (Judg. 17:5), and Solomon's father, David (1 Sam. 19:11–13). Some scholars argue that even Jacob could be added to the list because of the monument he built in Genesis 28:22. At the very least, he allowed his wife, Rachel, to keep idols among their possessions.

Finally, Solomon's idolatry led to idolatry among the people. They saw shrines to pagan gods being constructed on the hills around Jerusalem and knew that their king was championing a more diverse approach to spirituality. The only surprise would be if they *hadn't* gotten sucked into the practice of idolatry. When Elijah stepped to center stage after Solomon's reign ended, he found one of his biggest challenges to be idolatry among the people, in particular the worship of Baal.

Any one of these reasons would be enough for God to hate idol-atry. Add them together and you can begin to understand why the Bible refers to idols and idol worship as "detestable," "vile," "loathsome," "defiling," and "a disgrace." Perhaps you can also understand why God came down so hard on his people after the golden calf episode, with actions that the military would call "shock and awe." The Israelites were just getting started on their grand adventure, and they were going to be facing a land that was filled with false gods and graven images. God had to take a strong stand against idolatry, in much the same way you, as a parent, must meet that first point of rebellion in your child with a strong response.

WHAT DOES IDOLATRY LOOK LIKE TODAY?

Several years ago, a family visited our church for the first time. They hung around after the service so they could have a private moment with me. This is not particularly unusual. Sometimes families come to us in crisis and seek immediate help. But this was different. The head of the household's wife and children gathered around him bearing solemn expressions as he delivered God's judgment: our church was guilty of idolatry, and if we hoped to escape the fires of hell, we'd better repent.

Here's the backstory.

Our building features a thirty-foot ceiling in our foyer. That thirty-foot ceiling gives us a thirty-foot wall. Rather than leave that gigantic space empty, we had a Disney craftsman make us a cross, twenty feet tall and ten feet wide, to mount on that wall. It's made out of Styrofoam, but carved and painted to look like rough-hewn wood. It's light enough that a child could lift it but looks as though it would weigh a couple of tons. At any rate, it wasn't expensive, but it looks spectacular through the tall glass windows facing one of our county's busiest roads.

With his frowning family gathered around him, I asked the man why he believed we were guilty of idolatry. He said, "From the size of that cross in your foyer, it's obvious that you're all about the cross rather than the Christ."

As politely as possible, I explained that we have a big cross because we have a big wall. I said, "I can confidently tell you that the people who worship here are used to that cross and don't even see it or think about it when they come here. They're too busy worshipping and fellowshipping to give it a second thought. You can stand here week after week and watch the people come in and out of this building and you will see hardly a soul even glance up at the thing. It's purely a cosmetic touch, a piece of Christian art and nothing more."

He would have none of it.

He became agitated as he brought up the golden calf and started talking about graven images and God's punishment. I quickly shut the conversation down, assuring him that he had misjudged us and suggesting that if he attended our church for a while he would see that his accusation was unfounded. He said they would definitely *not* be attending our church again under any circumstances. I was at least gracious enough to wait until they left before I pumped my fist and said, "Thank you, Jesus!"

Okay, so what's the deal with crosses and pictures of Jesus and such? Are they idols? Are we going to hell if we have them in our homes or churches?

I believe it's good for every person to make their own decision on this, but a strong case can be made that Christian art is not only *not* bad but very good.

For one thing, consider that at the same time God gave Moses the first and second commandments, he also gave instructions for the building of the tabernacle. In that tabernacle were numerous items of ornate design that God instructed the Israelites to build. One of those items, the ark of the covenant, was made of acacia wood overlaid with gold and had elaborately carved cherubim on the lid.

Second, keep in mind that inside the ark of the covenant were several cherished objects, including the rod of Moses, a jar of manna, and the two stone tablets.

Finally, remember that when Solomon built the temple, he decorated it quite magnificently. First Kings 6:29–30 says, "He decorated all the walls of the inner sanctuary and the main room with carvings of cherubim, palm trees, and open flowers. He overlaid the floor in both rooms with gold."

What was God's response?

He said, "I have heard your prayer and your petition. I have set this Temple apart to be holy—this place you have built where my name will be honored forever. I will always watch over it, for it is dear to my heart" (1 Kings 9:3).

I believe we're barking up the wrong tree when we try to make the first and second commandments about crosses and pictures and other artistic expressions. In fact, I think Satan would love for us to make the first two commandments be about art so we would miss three deeper, more critical truths.

TRUTH #1: IDOLATRY CAN BE COMMITTED WITHOUT ANY PHYSICAL OBJECT BEING INVOLVED

Ananias and Sapphira, for example, appear to have made status their god. Remember when they lied to make themselves appear more generous than they really were (Acts 5:1–11)? Some scholars believe Ananias was jockeying for a position on the leadership team of the early church and talked his wife into playing along with a little scam that would make them look super spiritual.

King Saul of Israel was also a status worshipper. That's why he went ballistic after David killed Goliath and started receiving accolades from the people. "Saul has killed his thousands, and David his ten thousands!" the people sang, which infuriated Saul, a man who couldn't stand the thought of sharing the limelight with anyone.

And then there is our old friend Samson. Who can deny that his god was pleasure? The man had a weakness for women like a fish has a weakness for water. He also ate and drank outside the parameters of the Nazirite vow. In today's world he would likely be a porn addict or a serial adulterer, or both, and probably an alcoholic.

Clearly, a man's god can be just about anything from a carved statue to a long-held belief. It can be a position, a relationship, an image, a lifestyle, a feeling, or a career . . . anything that competes with God for first place in our lives.

TRUTH #2: IDOLATRY IS COMMON AMONG CHURCHGOERS

Don't think for a moment that idolatry is something only pagans do.

I know people who drive over an hour one way to attend a megachurch that has a famous preacher. During that one-hour weekly commute, they may well drive past twenty or thirty excellent, albeit smaller, churches that need their help and would provide them with greater convenience, blessed fellowship, and more opportunities to serve. But they're so enamored with the superstar preacher that they drive the extra miles to do nothing but sit in the audience and be wowed by their hero.

In a situation like this I think it's fair to ask who or what is being worshipped.

Or what about the church hopper who has attended five different churches in the last ten years? He and his family always arrive in their new church with beaming smiles and promises of loyalty. But at about the eighteen-month mark, the church's or the preacher's perceived imperfections start grating on their nerves. Suddenly, the sermons seem tedious and the music seems draggy and the people seem unspiritual, even though hundreds of other Christians are being blessed by the church's ministry. By the time the two-year mark rolls around, the man and his family are off to try a different church, explaining that they just weren't being fed.

In a situation like this I think it's fair to ask who or what is being worshipped.

Or what about the churchgoing couple who decides to go ahead and buy a house and move in together eight months before the wedding? They realize what the Bible says about fornication, but the house is both in their price range and in their neighborhood of choice. If they don't grab it, it'll be gone. And besides, by moving in together they can save money, which is good stewardship, is it not?

In a situation like this I think it's fair to ask who or what is being worshipped.

Or what about the associate minister who's been on the church staff for a few years? When his senior pastor decides to move on to another church, he feels his time has come, that he's paid his dues and deserves to be promoted to that lead position. But when the elders don't see him as a good fit and decide to hire someone else, he gets mad and resigns.

In a situation like this I think it's fair to ask who or what is being worshipped.

I could go on, but you get the idea.

Idolatry is often revealed not just in the choices we make but in the spirit in which we make them. Lots of churchgoers betray their allegiance to people and things other than Christ in the way they act.

TRUTH #3: IDOLATRY HAS BECOME EASIER WITH THE ADVANCE OF TECHNOLOGY

A man whose god is sexual pleasure can access all the porn he wants for free without leaving his house. Shopaholics can visit any store and buy any product at any hour of the day while sitting at their computers. Sports addicts can choose from an array of twenty-four-hour sports networks and watch several games simultaneously. Egomaniacs can promote themselves on YouTube and an ever-growing number of social media sites. Never in history have there been so many ways for obsessive people to indulge their fantasies and addictions.

Then again, sometimes I wonder if the technology itself hasn't become a god.

I've heard it said that you can tell what America worships by watching TV commercials. If that's true, then America certainly worships technology, because every other commercial seems to be advertising the latest smartphone, tablet, or app.

What troubles me is that there are people who simply cannot put their devices down. Not while they're driving, not while they're having dinner with the family, not even when they're in church. We have people who attend our church who wear their Bluetooth earpieces during the service. It's not unusual to hear a cell phone ring during the service and to see someone get up and walk out of the service to answer it.

In a situation like this I think it's fair to ask who or what is being worshipped.

The bottom line here is that idolatry is all around us. Bob Hostetler, in his fine book *American Idols*, wrote, "Our American idols may be harder to recognize than the worship of a stone idol.

They may also be harder to correct. But they are attitudes and life-styles that are abominations to God, and if we don't do something about them, they will corrupt and devastate us just as they did the Israelites in the wilderness of Sinai."[1] And, I might add, just as they did Solomon hundreds of years later.

HOW CAN WE GUARD AGAINST IDOLATRY?

SUGGESTION #1: FACE THE DANGER WITH NEW UNDERSTANDING

Far from being the one commandment we don't need to worry too much about, God's prohibition against worshipping other gods or graven images could well be the one we need to focus on first and foremost. Why? Because it's the thread through our popcorn.

Let me explain.

When I was a kid in VBS, our teacher's go-to craft project when she was fresh out of other ideas was to have us make the time-honored popcorn necklace. She would bring in a big bag of popcorn with some needles and thread. We would thread the needles and then push them through one piece of popcorn after another until we had a long string of popcorn. Then we'd tie the ends of the thread together and—*voila!*—a popcorn necklace!

So imagine that the popped kernels are our sins. Isn't idolatry the string that runs through them all? Isn't it true that every sin is, at least for that moment, an expression of devotion to something or someone other than the one true God?

Isn't it true that the man who looks at porn on the sly is putting something ahead of God?

What about the man who sleeps with his girlfriend?

The man who cheats on his taxes?

The man who pads his expense account?

The man who stretches the truth to make a sale?

The man who badmouths his competitor?

The man who doesn't pay his child support?

The man who cheats on his wife?

Aren't they all making a statement about whom or what is most important to them? You might say, "But what if it's just a one-time mistake?" Granted, it's better to cheat on your wife once than to cheat on her a hundred times. But isn't even one episode of cheating, for that moment at least, an idolatrous act?

When Solomon made his treaty with the Egyptian pharaoh and received the man's daughter as part of the deal, he did not think of it as an act of idolatry, but what else would you call it? He put political expediency ahead of God's clearly stated law. Even though many other ingredients in Solomon's life were ship-shape at that point, still, a little pinch of idolatry had been tossed into the mixing bowl.

The point is that we can't guard against idolatry if we are blind to it. We must understand that it is hiding in every temptation we face.

SUGGESTION #2: GUARD YOUR HEART WITH NEW VIGOR

Proverbs 4:23 says, "Guard your heart above all else, for it determines the course of your life." How do you guard your heart against idolatry? One way is to make sure God is a part of everything you do. Boy, that sounds cliché-ish, doesn't it? Like something you might hear at a platitude convention.

But think about it.

When we see Solomon at the height of his idolatrous lifestyle, marrying and buying and indulging like an out-of-control sailor on a weekend pass, what does he say over and over again?

"I said to myself . . ." (Eccl. 1:16).

"I said to myself . . ." (Eccl. 2:1).

"I said to myself . . ." (Eccl. 2:15).

"I said to myself . . ." (Eccl. 3:17).

"I said to myself . . ." (Eccl. 7:23).

Solomon was talking to himself about a lot of things he should have been discussing with God. Who can argue that the reason why he was seduced and eventually reduced to an object of scorn and pity was because he excluded God from so many areas of his life?

What other way is there to keep other people and things from edging out God except to start including God in everything you do?

Let's say you're going to buy a car. (You are aware, aren't you, that some people drive their idols? I know people who spend twice what they can afford just so they can drive a car that fits the image they want to project.) If you go with your impulse you could very easily be talked into buying a car that will feed your ego and fatally bleed your bank account. The last time I bought a car the salesman was showing me a luxury vehicle and said, "You deserve a car like this!" (A statement with huge idolatry implications!) But he didn't sucker me in because I had already prayed about my decision and settled on something I knew God and my wallet would both like. The salesman couldn't see him, but God was strolling the car lot with me that day.

Or let's say you're dating a girl. It's been a couple of months, things are going swimmingly, and now she is inviting you to take a trip with her to meet her grandma. A trip that will necessitate an overnight stay at a hotel. She says, "Don't worry, I'll make all the arrangements." The problem is, you don't know exactly what she's thinking: One room or two? If she's *not* thinking about one room, you don't want to insult her by asking if she is. On the other hand, if you don't ask and she makes a one-room reservation, the relationship could easily go places it's not ready to go. The answer, of course, is to invite God along on the trip by communicating from the get-go that you will go only if two rooms are booked.

Not only do I not know of a better way, I don't know of another way, period, to avoid idolatrous decisions than simply to make God a part of everything you do. Solomon eventually came to the same conclusion, for he said, "Trust in the LORD with all your heart; do not depend on your own understanding. *Seek his will in all you do*, and he will show you which path to take" (Prov. 3:5–6, author's emphasis).

Author Daniel Seagren said it this way: "Somehow, somewhere, someone must make it emphatic that God is not an add-on. When He permeates every aspect of our lives, our plans, our hopes, dreams, careers, vacations, and those times of stress and strain, we'll soon discover that He is not a meddlesome person to have around but an indispensable and very welcome presence."[2]

———

Going forward, understand that there's one throne in your heart. It's not a love seat, sofa, or sectional. It's one chair, offering room for only one person. Jesus has said that spot can't be shared (Matt. 6:24). You alone get to decide who or what sits in that space. The only way to guard against seduction is to give that place to God, and him alone.

WAKE-UP CALL №10

YOU KNOW YOU'RE BEING SEDUCED WHEN GOD DRAWS A BULL'S-EYE ON YOUR CHEST

HAPPY DAYS WAS ONE OF THE MOST POPULAR TELEVISION SHOWS of the 1970s and early '80s. Richie, Potsie, Ralph Malph, and Fonzie played out their shenanigans in front of an appreciative audience for eleven full seasons. During the premiere episode of the fifth season, there was a strange scene that showed a leather-jacketed Fonzie on water skis, jumping over a hungry shark. Critics and fans alike agree that the scene was so bad, so unfathomably awful, that it represents the show's worst moment. To this day, when people talk about something "jumping the shark," they're talking about that moment when everyone realizes rock bottom has been hit.

When did Solomon jump the shark? In my opinion, it was the day his construction team broke ground on the first pagan shrine. At that point, it was obvious to everyone—most of all God—that repentance was the furthest thing from Solomon's mind. Without question, it was going to take an intervention, some sort of life-shaking development to turn him around. And so God, with a sigh of sadness, did what he never *wants* to do but sometimes *has* to do. He drew a bull's-eye on Solomon's chest: "Then the LORD raised up Hadad the Edomite, a member of Edom's royal family, to be Solomon's adversary" (1 Kings 11:14).

And then nine verses later: "God also raised up Rezon son of Eliada as Solomon's adversary" (v. 23).

And then another three verses later: "Another rebel leader was Jeroboam son of Nebat, one of Solomon's own officials" (v. 26).

Suddenly, Solomon, the brilliant politician whose years of wheeling and dealing had resulted in more peace treaties than Hank Aaron has home runs, was finding the going considerably tougher. Adversaries were rising up from both inside and outside his administration, and they were rising up by the hand of God. Interestingly, while the most common English translations use the word *adversary* to describe these enemies, the original language allows for the word *satan*. Literally, God was raising up satans to oppose the man to whom he once said, "What do you want? Ask, and I will give it to you!" (1 Kings 3:5).

The reality here is stunning.

God has gone from letting Solomon take his pick from a vast smorgasbord of blessings to sending a trio of satans to make his life miserable. But it's not God who has changed; it's Solomon. From day one, God made it clear that his blessing depended on Solomon's faithfulness: "I will give you a wise and understanding heart such as no one else has had or ever will have! And I will also give you what you did not ask for—riches and fame! No other king in all the world will be compared to you for the rest of your life! And *if you follow me and obey my decrees and my commands* as your father, David, did, I will give you a long life" (vv. 12–14, author's emphasis).

And again: "As for you, *if you will follow me with integrity and godliness*, as David your father did, obeying all my commands, decrees, and regulations, then I will establish the throne of your dynasty over Israel forever" (1 Kings 9:4–5, author's emphasis).

THE BIGGEST WORD IN THE BIBLE

You see it in both of the passages you just read: the word *if*. It may not be the longest word in the Bible, but a strong case can be made that it's the biggest in terms of importance. It appears in Scripture almost two thousand times, and many of those times it sits there on the page making sure we don't forget that so much of what happens to us in life is our responsibility. Here are some more examples:

If the godly give in to the wicked,
    it's like polluting a fountain or muddying a spring. (Prov. 25:26)

If you ignore criticism, you will end in poverty and disgrace;
    if you accept correction, you will be honored. (Prov. 13:18)

My child, never forget the things I have taught you.
    Store my commands in your heart.
If you do this, you will live many years,
    and your life will be satisfying. (Prov. 3:1–2)

"Honor your father and mother." This is the first commandment with a promise: If you honor your father and mother, "things will go well for you, and you will have a long life on the earth." (Eph. 6:2–3)

If you keep yourself pure, you will be a special utensil for honorable use. Your life will be clean, and you will be ready for the Master to use you for every good work. (2 Tim. 2:21)

Time and time again the Bible writers dropped that word *if* into the text so that we would never forget how important our actions and choices are. I was recently reminded in a poignant way of how big this word is.

In our church office we have a handwritten, alphabetical listing of all the people who have ever been members of Poinciana Christian Church since the day it was first planted over thirty years ago. The list was started in a heavy ledger book back in the days before computers. Today, of course, we have all our records in a database. But for nostalgia's sake, we've kept that handwritten record up to date.

Not long ago, I was rummaging through a drawer and saw this book. It had been awhile since I'd thumbed through it, so I carried it into my office, sat down at my desk, and spent the next thirty minutes or so perusing its pages. Having been the minister of this church for almost twenty-five of its thirty-five years, I was able to put faces with most of the names. As you would expect, some of the people whose names I saw are no longer with us. Some are dead, a few moved or switched to a different church, but a significant number simply didn't remain faithful.

That was the part that got to me.

People whom I loved, whom I had fond memories of, whom I had witnessed to and baptized were, to put it as simply as I know how, not following the Lord anymore.

One name on the list was a man who accepted the Lord and was baptized in our church. I'll always remember his baptism because of a humorous glitch that occurred. That Sunday morning he was third in line to be baptized. However, our worship leader had a momentary mental lapse and struck up the worship band after the second baptism. When he realized the audience was laughing, the worship leader looked over his shoulder and saw that there was still one more baptism to come. He cut off the band and sheepishly stepped aside.

The young man I baptized at that moment had been in trouble with the law when he first walked through our doors, but with God's help he had straightened himself out and was living a great life. He used to tell me that he'd never been happier. Then he and his wife moved, and I lost track of him. Recently, I heard that he has dropped out of church and gone back to his old ways, even to the point of losing his marriage and getting involved with a married woman.

If you keep yourself pure . . .

If you remain faithful . . .

If you obey . . .

If . . .

If . . .

If . . .

In the end, it all comes down to that one little word.

Or rather, that one gigantic word.

It did for Solomon, and it will for you and me too.

THE TOUGHEST TRUTH IN THE BIBLE

There are many wonderful and heartwarming truths in the Bible, and a few that aren't so wonderful and heartwarming. One of the toughest truths for believers is that God does in fact draw bull's-eyes on his children's chests. If (there's that word again) one of his children is seduced and veers off into disobedience, God will do what any good father would do, and what he did for Solomon: take measures to bring the child back into line with his will.

Many years after Solomon wore a bull's-eye, the author of Hebrews wrote about how God's discipline works:

> "My child, don't make light of the LORD's discipline,
>   and don't give up when he corrects you.
> For the LORD disciplines those he loves,
>   and he punishes each one he accepts as his child."

As you endure this divine discipline, remember that God is treating you as his own children. Who ever heard of a child who is never disciplined by its father? If God doesn't discipline you as he does all of his children, it means that you are illegitimate and are not really his children at all. Since we respected our earthly fathers who disciplined us, shouldn't we submit even more to the discipline of the Father of our spirits, and live forever?

For our earthly fathers disciplined us for a few years, doing the best they knew how. But God's discipline is always good for us, so that we might share in his holiness. No discipline is enjoyable while it is happening—it's painful! But afterward there will be a peaceful harvest of right living for those who are trained in this way. (Heb. 12:5–11)

Here are five important facts about God's discipline every believer needs to understand.

FACT #1: GOD IS A "HANDS-ON" DISCIPLINARIAN

Parents take different approaches to discipline. Some negotiate with their kids, some take away privileges, and some (like my parents) take a more hands-on approach, if you know what I mean. The passage above makes it clear that God is a "hands-on" disciplinarian. In other words, his discipline stings.

Adam and Eve, who were banished from the garden of Eden, could attest to this.

So could their son Cain, who was cursed for murdering his brother.

So could Lot's wife, who was turned into a pillar of salt for looking back at Sodom.

So could Miriam, who was given leprosy for criticizing.

So could Achan, who was struck dead for stealing.

So could Ananias and Sapphira, who were struck dead for lying.

God is no pussyfooter when it comes to discipline. He understands that inflicted pain can accomplish what no amount of harping or haranguing can. Proverbs 20:30 says, "Physical punishment cleanses away evil; such discipline purifies the heart."

This should make you stop and think.

Are you involved in some activity that you know God disapproves of? Perhaps an inappropriate relationship or some dishonesty at work? If so, you need to understand that you are inviting God to take painful action against you. Don't think that because you're a pastor or a small group leader or some other kind of kingdom servant God will take it easy on you. Even of David, the man after God's own heart, God said, "I will be his father, and he will be my son. If he sins, I will correct and discipline him with the rod, like any father would do" (2 Sam. 7:14).

FACT #2: GOD IS MORE CONCERNED ABOUT YOUR DIRECTION THAN YOUR SIN

God doesn't generally respond immediately to the sins of his people. Solomon, for example, accumulated a thousand wives and concubines before God started raising up adversaries to make his life miserable. Most scholars believe at least a year went by after David committed adultery with Bathsheba before God stepped up and took action against him. Even in the case of Ananias and Sapphira, whom God struck dead for lying, there could have been prior offenses we're not told about.

The reason God generally doesn't start drawing bull's-eyes and slinging lightning bolts at us as soon as we mess up is because he expects us to sin. Psalm 103:13–14 says, "The LORD is like a father to his children, tender and compassionate to those who fear him. For he knows how weak we are; he remembers we are only dust."

I was recently reminded of how meaningful these words are.

Some parents who were frustrated with their junior high–age son came to see me. They went on and on about how they couldn't get him to "shape up." His room was too messy to suit them, his appearance too scruffy, and his attitude too lackadaisical. His mother, in full exasperation mode, said, "He just drives me crazy with his earbuds and his shuffling around." But I noticed that there was nothing really evil in what the kid was doing. So when they asked me what I thought, I said, "Honestly, I think he's perfectly normal. Don't forget, he's thirteen years old. I suspect there are a lot of parents of thirteen-year-olds that would be thrilled if their kids were like yours."

God never forgets that we're thirteen years old, so to speak. He never forgets that we're made of dust. So when we sin, he doesn't immediately marshal his troops and send them marching off to make war against us. He notices, for sure. He's displeased, absolutely. He feels the pain of it, no doubt. But he understands how weak we are, that we *are* going to sin.

It's the direction of our lives that concerns him most of all. Haven't you noticed how often the Bible talks about the life of faith being a path or a highway or a road that we follow? For example, Proverbs 15:24 says, "The path of life leads upward for the wise." And Matthew 7:14: "The gateway to life is very narrow and the road is difficult, and only a few ever find it." God's discipline is most likely to be visited upon us not when we commit an isolated sin but when we depart from the path of righteousness and go off in a completely different direction. That's what Solomon did.

FACT #3: GOD IS ON YOUR SIDE, EVEN WHEN HE'S DISCIPLINING YOU

In the case of Solomon, God was raising up adversaries to hassle him, but when those skirmishes occurred, God was anything but an unbiased observer. He was on Solomon's side all the way! I can see him actively rooting for Solomon not just to defend the kingdom but to wake up and realize how his life had changed for the worse.

Isn't this the whole point of discipline? As a parent, you're hoping the disciplinary action you take will cause your child not just to change his behavior but to rethink his behavior.

When I was a kid, I was disciplined much more severely than most of my friends. One time when I was in high school, I hit a lousy shot on the golf course and angrily flung my club down the fairway. It was quite an impressive throw, actually. It spun horizontally through the air like a helicopter for about thirty yards. My dad's response was to confiscate my golf clubs for two weeks. And you have to understand, this was at a time when I was obsessed with golf. I would rather have had him deprive me of nourishment than take away my clubs. But it was during that time of golf deprivation (when my brother, who was the model of decorum, was still playing up a storm) that I was forced to ask myself the hard question: *How did I get myself into this situation?* This, of course, was exactly the question my father was hoping I'd ask myself. I'm sure he was praying, "Lord, help him get the message."

I haven't thrown a club since.

As Hadad and Rezon and Jeroboam were hassling Solomon, God was rooting for the king to get the message, to think back on those not-too-distant days when he had no enemies at all, and to reflect on what had changed.

Let me explain why this point is so important.

A lot of Christians, when they suffer, immediately assume that God has abandoned them. I hear it all the time: "Where is God? It's like he's deserted me, or even worse, turned against me." And they don't stop to think that maybe the suffering they're experiencing is actually loving, parental discipline coming from the hand of the very God they assume has vanished. That's why I always challenge suffering people with some hard questions. Have you gotten lazy in your spiritual life? Have you let some sin creep in? Are you hiding something?

Hebrews 12:6–7 says, "'For the LORD disciplines those he loves, and he punishes each one he accepts as his child.' As you endure this divine discipline, remember that God is treating you as his own children." It is always a mistake to equate new suffering with some failure on God's part. Because God is always on your side, the first question you ask should be of yourself: *Am I doing something that would make my heavenly Father feel the need to discipline me?*

FACT #4: GOD IS MORE CONCERNED ABOUT YOUR REPENTANCE THAN YOUR COMFORT

Perhaps the greatest biblical example of this is in Numbers 21:

Then the people of Israel set out from Mount Hor, taking the road to the Red Sea to go around the land of Edom. But the people grew impatient with the long journey, and they began to speak against God and Moses. "Why have you brought us out of Egypt to die here in the wilderness?" they complained. "There is nothing to eat here and nothing to drink. And we hate this horrible manna!" (vv. 4–5)

I doubt that many of us would rank bellyaching very high on a list of offensive sins, but God apparently does, because he fashioned the mother of all disciplinary actions to deal with the Israelites' complaining: "So the LORD sent poisonous snakes among the people, and many were bitten and died" (v. 6). This passage has always given me the creeps. If you recall, the very first line of chapter 1 of this book is: *I hate snakes, probably more than anybody you've ever met.* When I read this passage about snakes infiltrating the Israelites' camp, I know without a doubt that the comfort of his people is not God's number one priority. To be blunt, he doesn't mind terrorizing his people if it will lead them to repentance. In the case of the Israelites, they did repent, and pronto. (Who wouldn't?) The very next verse has the people running to Moses and confessing their sins.

Proverbs 9:10 says, "Fear of the LORD is the foundation of wisdom." I know there are people who say that the word *fear* is interchangeable with the word *respect*, that we should never be afraid of God in the traditional sense.

Sorry, I'm not buying it.

When I read about God sending a plague of poisonous snakes to bite and kill his people, I realize he will do whatever it takes to trigger our repentance.

Whatever. It. Takes.

Yes, I believe God wants me to pull back from sin out of a desire to be faithful. But on those days when I can't muster that desire, I believe God is perfectly content for me to pull back from sin because I am scared to death of the disciplinary action he might take.

FACT #5: GOD ALWAYS HAS HIS FOOT ON THE BRAKE

My uncle Carl Pankey was one of the most unusual men I've ever known. A professional golfer who played with the likes of

Sam Snead and Arnold Palmer, he eventually settled into life as a small-town club pro in Fairfield, Illinois. He was one of only two people I've ever ridden in a car with who was a two-footed driver. That is, he worked the brake with his left foot and the gas with his right—often at the same time! My brother and I rode to a PGA tournament with him one time, and we both about had whiplash by the time we got home.

You could say that God is also a two-footed driver. Yes, he can stomp down on the gas, as the plague of poisonous snakes clearly proves. But his foot is always on the brake, ready and willing to call a halt to the pain when repentance happens. God made this clear to Solomon after the dedication of the newly constructed temple and palace: "If my people who are called by my name will humble themselves and pray and seek my face and turn from their wicked ways, I will hear from heaven and will forgive their sins and restore their land" (2 Chron. 7:14).

Even as God was raising up adversaries to go against Solomon, there's no doubt God would have squashed those enemies as fast as he raised them up if Solomon had fallen on his face and repented.

What an important truth this is for us to remember.

If you sense that the suffering that has come into your life is God's response to your sin, there's something you can do about it! It's like when I was a kid. When I misbehaved, my mom would plop my fanny in a chair and say, "You're going to sit there until you decide to behave." She could have said, "You're going to sit there for an hour." But no, she made it clear that the whole point of the exercise was to bring about a change in my behavior. When that happened, the purpose would be served and there would be no more need for me to suffer. Simply put, her foot was on the brake, just waiting for me to give her a reason to press it.

———

I want to close this chapter with some simple advice on how to determine if the suffering you're experiencing is God's discipline or not. I've gotten this question from a lot of hurting people over the years: "Am I just experiencing life in a fallen world or has God drawn a bull's-eye on my chest?" I would suggest that the trouble you're experiencing just might be God's discipline if one or more of the following possibilities is true.

POSSIBILITY #1: THERE IS UNTENDED SIN IN YOUR LIFE

As I said earlier in this chapter, God doesn't generally lower the boom on us because we commit one sin. But when we allow sin to take root and grow—when the path of our lives veers off in the wrong direction—he is likely to respond. This, of course, was Solomon's problem. It was also Samson's problem and David's problem, two other guys who felt God's disciplinary sting.

Is it also your problem?

Keep in mind, the sin in question doesn't have to be of the headline-making variety. It might be quite small by the world's standards. It might even be some small thing you've stopped doing rather than something you've started doing. Jesus made it clear that the small sins are critical when he said, "If you are dishonest in little things, you won't be honest with greater responsibilities" (Luke 16:10). What might God be seeing that he wants cleaned out of your life?

POSSIBILITY #2: THE TROUBLE YOU'RE FACING IS ATYPICAL

The grief that Hadad, Rezon, and Jeroboam brought into Solomon's life was atypical, to say the least. He'd been sailing along with no significant enemies whatsoever for a long time. The very fact that trouble had erupted in such a traditionally peaceful area of his life should have raised some questions in his mind.

Of course, new trouble doesn't always indicate God's discipline.

Sometimes factors we have nothing to do with, such as a cranky new boss or a sinking economy, can trigger problems we haven't faced before. Nevertheless, it's always wise to scrutinize new trouble to see if there's a discernible reason why it has suddenly cropped up.

POSSIBILITY #3: THE SOURCE OF YOUR PRIDE/ PLEASURE IS THE CENTER OF YOUR TROUBLE

This was certainly the case with Solomon. The source of both his pride and his pleasure was his wealth and power, which is exactly what was under attack when Hadad, Rezon, and Jeroboam launched their campaigns against him. And keep in mind, there was nothing wrong with Solomon being wealthy or powerful. Those were gifts God had given him. The problem was that he had begun taking those blessings for granted. Instead of remembering that God had granted them because of his faithfulness and had promised to take them away if he was unfaithful, Solomon started acting like he was entitled to them—like he could do anything he wanted with impunity, including building shrines to false gods.

What gives you pride and pleasure? Whatever it is, you can bet Satan has identified that area of your life as a vulnerability. He may use it to blow up your ego or compromise your principles or divert your attention away from important spiritual disciplines, which, in turn, could cause God to step in and have his say.

With all of this in mind, I don't know of any way to be absolutely certain 100 percent of the time if a particular spot of trouble is God's discipline or just the normal wear and tear of life. We do know, however, that God does discipline his children and that his discipline is painful. That being the case, I believe the only sensible thing for any Christian to do when trouble comes is to explore this possibility first. Examine yourself. Pray and ask God to search your heart and reveal anything that might be amiss. And if something turns up, get busy and fix it.

If only Solomon had done this, how different his life and legacy would have been.

AFTERWORD

THIS IS NOW THE THIRD BOOK I'VE WRITTEN THAT IS AN IN-DEPTH study of a Bible character. Every time, as I've come to the end of such a project, the same question has occurred to me: What would the person have to say about his own life? If he could magically appear before us today, what insights, explanations, or excuses would he offer? In the cases of Samson and Caleb (my other two subjects), we'll never know. But in the case of Solomon, we do, for Solomon lived long enough to give us the book of Ecclesiastes, which many scholars believe was written during the last four or five years of his life.

If you've read Ecclesiastes, you know that its tone is very bleak. Words like *vanity*, *meaningless*, *folly*, and *foolish* are sprinkled throughout the text. Though it appears that Solomon had finally come to his senses, you can't escape the feeling that the seduction of his soul had taken a terrible toll, that he was significantly reduced in ways that age alone could not accomplish.

In Ecclesiastes 7:29, reflecting on his life and experience,

Solomon said, "But I did find this: God created people to be virtuous, but they have each turned to follow their own downward path." I am intrigued by those last ten words: "they have each turned to follow their own downward path."

We're all sinners, of course. But is it true that we each have our own downward paths? That is to say, a specially designed path that leads away from God, one that has been meticulously tailored by Satan to fit our own unique needs, fears, longings, and weaknesses? And if so, what hope do we have of resisting this path? If Solomon, the wisest man who ever lived, was seduced by his own downward path, can we even hope to avoid ours?

I believe the answers are yes and yes.

Yes, we all have our own downward paths.

And yes, we can hope to avoid them.

If I didn't believe this, I wouldn't have spent a year of my life writing this book.

I'm convinced that the key to avoiding your own downward path is simply to heed life's wake-up calls. As I've tried to show you, those wake-up calls were constantly sounding in Solomon's life. They came from circumstances, problems, enemies, and even the mouth of God himself. Solomon could've responded to any of them at any point along the way. He didn't, but he could've.

And so can we.

The apostle John said, "The Spirit who lives in you is greater than the spirit who lives in the world" (1 John 4:4). Who is the spirit who lives in the world? He's the designer, the paver, and the maintainer of your own downward path. John says that if you're a Christian, he is inferior, even impotent, compared to the Spirit of God who lives in you.

It makes me sad that Solomon was seduced so thoroughly, that he so willingly followed his own downward path. You can tell from the book of Ecclesiastes that it made him sad too. But just because he did, doesn't mean we have to. My prayer is that you'll be fully awake and fully determined to move forward on your own *upward* path.

A MESSAGE FROM MARK

I'M NOT THE KIND OF PERSON WHO LOOKS FOR SIGNS. HOWEVER, I couldn't help noticing that on the day I finished the last chapter of this book, there were three stories in the news about prominent men who were caught up in scandals. One was a well-known preacher whose wife was divorcing him because of his alleged unfaithfulness to their marriage vows. Those stories had the weird, dual effect of making me both sad and happy. Sad that the men and their families were suffering such pain, but happy that I had taken the time to write a book that might help someone somewhere avoid a similar fate. That is my prayer for this work, pure and simple.

As always, I want to express my sincere appreciation to you, my readers, for the time you spent with this book. I know you're busy and that there are countless other books to which you could have devoted that time. I would love to hear your comments, questions, and testimonies. You can e-mail me at MarkAtteberry@aol. com. I am committed to answering every e-mail.

I also want you to know about my blog. I've designed it as an online devotional. Twice a week I post a devotion that you can read in two minutes. Though short, my devos are packed with little-known historical facts, anecdotes, social commentary, humor, and, yes, lots of Scripture. I've been told that some small groups are using the devos as discussion starters. If you subscribe, the posts will show up in your e-mail automatically. You can find my blog at alittlestrongereveryday.com.

I'd also like to connect with you on Facebook. To be honest, I still haven't decided if Facebook is a blessing or a curse, but it gives me a simple way to connect with my readers and that, at least, is a good thing.

Thank you again for meeting me in the pages of this book. I'm already hard at work on the next one. Perhaps it will bring us together again. I hope so.

Mark Atteberry

STUDY GUIDE

*Questions for Personal Study
or Group Discussion*

WAKE-UP CALL №1: SIN SEEMS LIKE A GOOD IDEA

1. Tell about a time when a sinful act seemed like a good idea. Who or what, if anything, was influencing you at the time?
2. Many scholars believe that Solomon did not propose or initiate the alliance with Egypt that resulted in him taking his first foreign wife. Do you believe this mitigates his guilt to any degree? Is the person who follows someone into sin less guilty than the person who leads someone into sin?
3. The "lipsticks" Satan uses to make sin look harmless and attractive are alcohol, privacy, financial benefit, popular opinion, moderation, and peer participation. Which of these have fooled you? How would you rank them in terms of their effectiveness?
4. Name a bit of discernment you learned the hard way (through a painful experience). Do you believe lessons learned the hard way stick with you better? Why do you

think some people continue to have painful experiences without ever learning their lessons?

5. Turn to page 14 and calculate your dupability quotient. What do you think this says about you? Do you believe Satan sees you as an easy target or a tough nut to crack? What changes could you undertake that would make you harder to deceive?

WAKE-UP CALL №2: GOD'S COMMANDS SEEM OUT OF TOUCH

1. "Scripture is a Christian's first line of defense." Do you agree or disagree with this statement? How would you rate your own knowledge of and commitment to God's Word? What are you currently doing to increase your knowledge of Scripture?

2. Solomon's seduction began with what seemed to be a small deviation from God's will (taking an Egyptian wife). Can you think of an occasion when you made what seemed to be a small deviation from God's will, only to have it turn into a big problem? Is there really any such thing as a "small" deviation from God's will?

3. One of Solomon's problems was that his priorities became muddled. What worldly priorities began to crowd out the simple priority of obeying God? Take a moment and think about your own priorities. Have they evolved over time? If so, have they moved in a more spiritual or less spiritual direction? Explain.

4. Solomon's advisors failed him. Who are your primary advisors in life? Have you ever removed a person from your circle of friends because you felt he or she was a

negative influence in your life? What qualities should a confidant or advisor possess?

5. Solomon's life story illustrates that only a slight change of direction can result in a dramatic change in destination. Think back to the time when you first started following the Lord. Considering your commitment to the spiritual disciplines, your church attendance, your stewardship, and the general health of your relationships, would you say that your direction changed at all? If so, what needs to change so you can get back on the main path of faith and obedience?

WAKE-UP CALL №3: YOUR GLORY IS MORE IMPORTANT TO YOU THAN GOD'S GLORY

1. Between 1 Kings 3 and 1 Kings 8, there is a dramatic increase in the size of Solomon's ego. What are some things that typically result in someone growing more arrogant? Are any of those factors present in your life? Have you ever had someone accuse you of being arrogant or egotistical? If so, do you feel that accusation was justified? Why?

2. Because so many big-ego people are highly successful, there are people who claim that having a big ego is a key to success in life. Can you name a highly successful person who doesn't have a big ego? In your opinion, what are the signs that an ego has gotten too big?

3. According to 1 Kings 6:37–7:1, it took Solomon almost twice as long to build his house as it did to build God's house. How conscious are you of appearances when it comes to material things? When you buy a house, a car, or clothing, what are your priorities? Have you ever been guilty of overspending in an effort to project a certain

image? If so, can you name specific ways the overspending benefited you?

4. It's been said that *ego* stands for "Edging God Out." Based
on Solomon's experience and your own observations, in
what specific areas of an egotistical person's life is God
likely to get edged out? Can you think of other Bible characters whose egos created a problem between themselves
and God?

5. Jesus said that whoever wants to be first must become a
slave. Generally speaking, do you believe Christians in our
generation have embraced or rejected this truth? Can you
point to specific evidence that *you* have embraced this truth?

WAKE-UP CALL №4: YOU'RE MORE INFLUENCED BY ENTICEMENTS THAN WARNINGS

1. "Virtually all the messes we get ourselves into are the
result of us ignoring warnings. Not *missing* them, but
ignoring them." Can you think of a time when you got
into trouble by ignoring a warning? If so, why did you do
it? Did you ever make that same mistake again? Can you
name some warnings that did cause you to change course?

2. Have you ever used the "God just wants me to be happy"
excuse for sin? Has anyone ever used it on you? Granting
that God does indeed want his children to be happy,
what's wrong with this statement?

3. Things that used to be taboo (like cohabitation and erotic
literature) have gone mainstream in our culture to the
point that a lot of Christians are indulging. What is your
opinion of your church's voice on such matters? Has it
been too quiet? Too obnoxious in its opposition? What

about your own voice? Do you speak up when you have an opportunity to share God's will on such matters?

4. God's warnings are very specific. Every sin Solomon committed was a violation of a plainly stated law. Can you remember a time when you broke a law of God that was clearly stated and that you understood perfectly well? What do you believe is behind this kind of disobedience?

5. In Jeremiah 16:17 God said, "I am watching them closely, and I see every sin. They cannot hope to hide from me." To what extent do you sense God watching you as you go about your daily business? Do you think of God's constant observation of you negatively (as if he's intruding) or positively (as if he's protecting you)? Has your knowledge of his constant watching ever stopped you from committing a sin?

WAKE-UP CALL №5: SIN MANAGEMENT SEEMS LIKE A BETTER CHOICE THAN REPENTANCE

1. In spite of the many complications it brings, countless people find sin management to be a more attractive option than total repentance. Why do you think this is? Have you ever tried to hang on to a sin by cleverly managing it? How did it turn out?

2. First John 2:15 says, "Do not love this world nor the things it offers you, for when you love the world, you do not have the love of the Father in you." How do you reconcile this verse with the fact that we all love things in this world, whether it's music, sports, books, our jobs, or even our families? Evaluate Solomon's life in the light of this verse. He obviously loved worldly things. Do you think he had the love of the Father in him? Explain your answer.

3. Compartmentalizing sin seemed like a good idea to Solomon, as it does to many men today. What would be some of the dangers of compartmentalization from a purely logistical standpoint? What would be some of the dangers from a spiritual standpoint? Can you think of some people whose lives were seriously damaged because they chose to compartmentalize rather than repent? Have you ever been burned by doing this? If so, what didn't you take into account when you decided to try it?

4. Jerry Sandusky, former assistant football coach at Penn State, managed his pedophilia successfully for years. What lessons could be drawn from his ability to accomplish this? At what point should a conscientious person "blow the whistle" on a sin manager?

5. Repentance concerns itself with how things *are*, while sin management only worries about how things *look*. Right now, is there an area of your life that looks good to the people around you, but only because you've managed your sin so well? If so, what components of your deception could fall apart? What damage would be done to you and your loved ones if they did? What is stopping you from simply repenting and getting the sin out of your life completely?

WAKE-UP CALL №6: YOUR FAITHFUL FRIENDS ARE TROUBLED BY YOUR BEHAVIOR

1. Solomon's friendship with Hiram suffered a serious blow after being rock solid for twenty years. Have you ever had a longtime friendship go bad? If so, what happened? What did you learn from the experience?

2. Testosterone commercials that show middle-aged men

worrying about their libidos are one way pressure is put on men to live up to a certain cultural standard. In what other ways have you felt that pressure? Have you suffered any guilt or inferiority as a result of this pressure? Have you made any changes to your lifestyle in an effort to be more of what culture suggests you should be? If so, how have these changes affected you and your relationships?

3. The suspicion trigger for Hiram, the thing that told him something was awry in his relationship with Solomon, had to do with a change in their business relationship. Have you ever lost a friendship in a dispute over money or business? How do the dynamics of a relationship change when money gets involved? In general, do you think it's wise for friends to go into business together?

4. Has a friend ever approached you about a negative change in your attitude or behavior? If so, what was your reaction? Did that confrontation help or harm your relationship? Have you ever approached someone in this way? What was the result?

5. "In my experience, there's no human being more pitiful than the man who has destroyed his most precious possession, only to realize it after the damage was done." Is there a relationship you cherish that is under stress right now because of you? If so, what can you do to relieve that stress before permanent damage is done?

WAKE-UP CALL №7: YOUR DRINKING GLASSES COST MORE THAN SOME PEOPLE'S HOUSES

1. "Materialism isn't about your balance sheet; it's about your heart." Think about the things in life that are important to you. How many of them are material? To

what extent does your happiness and self-esteem revolve around those material things? Are you conscious of how you measure up to others with regard to material things?

2. We are born with an affinity for materialism. How was that affinity encouraged or discouraged by the people who raised you? If you're a parent, how careful are you to teach your children about the dangers of materialism? Specifically, how do you do it?

3. Solomon assumed his happiness would grow right along with his wealth, but it didn't. Do you know anyone who's become less happy as he has become wealthier? Why do you think this so often happens? What are some of the things people believe about being wealthy that turn out not to be true?

4. When it comes to money and material things, how much of a risk taker are you? Are you drawn toward high-risk investments? Do you play the lottery? Gamble? Have you ever let a friend talk you into doing something risky with your money? If so, what do you think that says about you?

5. How would you rate yourself when it comes to generosity? Do you tithe to your church? Do you support charitable causes? Or are you a hoarder? Solomon said, "There is another serious problem I have seen under the sun. Hoarding riches harms the saver" (Eccl. 5:13). Have you experienced this? What is it about hoarding riches that is so appealing to people?

WAKE-UP CALL №8: THERE ARE A THOUSAND WOMEN LINED UP OUTSIDE YOUR BATHROOM

1. "Solomon wasn't the first or the last man to let the love of a woman (or women) turn him into a fool." Has the love

of a woman ever turned you into a fool? If so, at what
point did you realize that you had crossed the border and
entered the land of fools? You obviously went there willingly. Can you explain why?

2. Are you a flirt? Or if not a flirt, do you just enjoy being
   around women? Do you have lots of female friends? Are
   there women you confide in and who confide in you? If
   so, explain why you believe this is not dangerous. (I'm
   assuming you don't think it's dangerous since you have
   allowed the situation to develop.)

3. If you're married, is there another woman who has grown
   more attractive to you than your wife? What is it about
   her that draws your interest? Do you fantasize about being
   in a relationship with her? If you were in a relationship
   with her, do you believe she would be able to maintain
   that aura of perfection? What flaws do you see in her that
   you would find troublesome in a real-life relationship?
   What qualities does your wife possess that compelled you
   to marry her but that now seem less important? Why do
   you think your feelings have changed?

4. Given that Tiger Woods, Anthony Weiner, Brett Favre,
   and others have been embarrassed and shamed by inappropriate text messages, consider your own use of texting
   and social media. If all your e-mails and texts were
   flashed on a screen for the world to see, would you feel
   proud or humiliated? Why do you think so many otherwise intelligent males use such bad judgment in this area?

5. Considering the fact that Jesus said adultery need not
   involve physical contact (Matt. 5:28), is it possible that
   you have become an adulterer without actually having an
   illicit sexual relationship? What does the term "emotional
   affair" mean to you? Is there a friendship in your life that

is tainted by sexually charged feelings? If so, why haven't you ended, or at least adjusted, that relationship to bring it in line with God's will?

WAKE-UP CALL №9: THE THRONE OF YOUR HEART GOES FROM BEING A CHAIR TO A SOFA TO A SECTIONAL

1. "I couldn't live without my _____." If you've spoken those words, how did you fill in the blank? Is there some material possession you value so much that your happiness would be profoundly affected if you lost it? How do you view this in light of the Bible's warnings about idols?

2. Are you currently compromising your faith in some area of your life? Have you lowered your spiritual standards to accommodate a desire or a goal that is important to you? Are you willing to acknowledge that this is idolatry? Given God's well-documented hatred of idolatry, are you willing to stop making those compromises?

3. The apostle Paul connects idols and demons (1 Cor. 10:19–20). What has been your attitude toward demons in the past? Do you think it's possible that in our age of education and sophistication, demonic activity could subtly creep into our lives through our love for possessions or money or status?

4. "How do you guard your heart against idolatry? One way is to make sure God is a part of everything you do." Is there an area of your life from which God has been excluded? What about your sex life? (Are you into porn or living promiscuously?) Your financial life? (Do you disdain tithing?) Your entertainment choices? (Are you into

godless music, violent video games, or vulgar movies?) If there is an area of your life that has been off-limits to God, are you willing to make the profound changes that would be required to let him back in? What would those changes look like?

5. Do you think it's possible for a churchgoing person with no blatantly sinful habits to be an idol worshipper? What kind of idols might a stereotypical "good little Christian" have? Do you believe idols that come wrapped in religious packaging are less dangerous, more dangerous, or about as dangerous as worldly idols? Explain why.

WAKE-UP CALL №10: GOD DRAWS A BULL'S-EYE ON YOUR CHEST

1. Does it trouble you to think about God raising up adversaries to make Solomon's life miserable? Why do you think God waited so long?

2. Have you ever had the feeling that God was after you—that he had drawn a bull's-eye on your chest and was coming to take you down? If so, what was happening to make you feel that way? Did you know why he was after you? Did you change whatever it was you felt had displeased him?

3. "God is more concerned about your direction than your sin." What is the direction of your life right now? Are you closer to the Lord and more obedient than you were a year ago? Are you more patient and generous? Are your relationships in better shape? If not, to what do you attribute the decline? Have you thought about the fact that you might be inviting God's discipline into your life?

4. Do you think God is pleased or displeased when our righteousness is primarily driven by our fear of his discipline? Explain. If you're a parent, how do you feel when you know it's only the fear of punishment that keeps your child from disobeying?

5. The suffering that Solomon experienced because of God's discipline was atypical. His reign had been characterized by peaceful relations with foreign kings, but suddenly they were attacking him. Is there some new suffering that has recently come into your life? If so, what do you attribute it to? Is there a responsibility in that area of your life that you have failed to maintain? Or perhaps a bad habit that has crept in? If so, how do you plan to address it?

ACKNOWLEDGMENTS

I'M NOT THE MOST PROLIFIC AUTHOR IN THE WORLD, BUT I'VE written enough books to know the difference between a good publishing experience and a bad one. The crew at Thomas Nelson Publishers—Matt Baugher, Adria Haley, Kevin Harvey, and Andrea Lucado—never once wrinkled my brow. All the way through I kept thinking, *It should be harder than this.* I want to thank them for their kindness and professionalism.

I'm also grateful for Lee Hough's vision and cheerleading. He was gung-ho for this book from the moment I bounced the idea off him. I'm convinced that no man ever had a better agent or friend. Lee died shortly after I finished this manuscript, leaving a large void in the lives of many. I will always remember him as a man of steadfast faith who cared about authors a lot more than he cared about the books they wrote.

Dr. Les Hardin, professor at Johnson University, is my go-to guy when I get stuck on a difficult verse or a thorny theological issue. He responds to my e-mails quickly and in depth. Everybody should have a friend who is ten times smarter than they are. Les is that friend to me.

The members of Poinciana Christian Church have allowed me to be their preacher for the last twenty-four years. Why, I can't say. Surely they know they could do better. But I am grateful for their unwavering love and support.

My daughter, Michelle, and her two kids, Alyssa and Alexis, had absolutely nothing to do with the writing or the publication of this book. But I love them so much I want to mention them. When Alyssa and Alexis grow up, I know they'll think it's cool that their names are mentioned here.

Finally, my wife, Marilyn, is a great author's wife. Authors are quirky, as any author's spouse will tell you. She puts up with my blank stares, crazy hours, lightning-bolt ideas, and rambling brainstorm sessions without complaint. I especially appreciate how she pretends it's all perfectly normal.

ABOUT THE AUTHOR

MARK ATTEBERRY IS THE AWARD-WINNING AUTHOR OF ELEVEN books and dozens of articles. You can follow him @mark_atteberry and read his blog at at alittlestrongereveryday.com. Since 1989, he has served as the preaching minister at Poinciana Christian Church in Kissimmee, Florida. When he isn't writing or preaching, Mark enjoys being a husband, father, and grandfather, and pursuing a variety of interests, including sports, playing the sax, and collecting jazz records.

NOTES

WAKE-UP CALL #1: SIN SEEMS LIKE A GOOD IDEA
1. Jon Sandys, *Movie Mistakes* (London: Virgin Books, 2002), 27.
2. John Assaraf and Murray Smith, *The Answer* (New York: Atria Books, 2008), 36.

WAKE-UP CALL #2: GOD'S COMMANDS SEEM OUT OF TOUCH
1. John W. Loftus, *The Christian Delusion* (New York: Prometheus Books, 2010), 202.
2. Steven Covey, *The Speed of Trust* (New York: Free Press, 2006), 63.

WAKE-UP CALL #3: YOUR GLORY IS MORE IMPORTANT TO YOU THAN GOD'S GLORY
1. Ken Blanchard and Phil Hodges, *Lead Like Jesus* (Nashville: Thomas Nelson, 2005), 42.

WAKE-UP CALL #5: SIN MANAGEMENT SEEMS LIKE A BETTER CHOICE THAN REPENTANCE
1. John Vawter, *Uncommon Graces* (Colorado Springs: NavPress, 1998), 123–24.

WAKE-UP CALL #7: YOUR DRINKING GLASSES COST MORE THAN SOME PEOPLE'S HOUSES

1. Alexander Green, *The Gone Fishin' Portfolio* (Hoboken, NJ: John Wiley & Sons, 2008), 36.
2. Bonnie Kavoussi, "Number of PhD Recipients Using Food Stamps Surged During Recession: Report," *Huffington Post*, May 8, 2012, http://www.huffingtonpost.com/2012/05/07/food -stamps-phd-recipients-2007-2010_n_1495353.html.

WAKE-UP CALL #9: THE THRONE OF YOUR HEART GOES FROM BEING A CHAIR TO A SOFA TO A SECTIONAL

1. Bob Hostetler, *American Idols* (Nashville: Broadman & Holman, 2006), 17.
2. Daniel R. Seagren, *Love Carved in Stone* (Ventura, CA: Regal Books, 1983), 28.